FORTRESS OF STEEL

Legion of the Damned
Book One

Jeff Jones

Also in the Legion of the Damned Series

Forests of Death

Islands of Mist

The Hunt For Boudica

Tides of Blood

FORTRESS OF STEEL

Published by Sapere Books.

24 Trafalgar Road, Ilkley, LS29 8HH

saperebooks.com

ISBN: 978-0-85495-687-6

To Jackie,
Thank you for believing.

ACKNOWLEDGEMENTS

It has long been a dream of mine to see Centurion Corvo and his comrades march out of my already overpopulated head and onto the page, and I would like to thank Amy Durant, Caoimhe O'Brien and everyone at Sapere Books who has made this dream a reality.

Thanks also to all those who have supported me over the years and provided invaluable feedback and encouragement — my family and all the short story writers and editors I have interacted with over the years. Thanks also to Emily Dixon for her help in dragging me into the twenty-first century by building me a website.

Finally, a special thank you to Sarah Luddington and Fraser Simpson, the former for moral support and the odd kick up the backside, and the latter for his unswerving encouragement and praise, even when it was not warranted … gratitude!

CHAPTER 1

Rome, AD 59

Centurion Marcus Ovidius Corvo instinctively flinched in his seat in the front row as the gladiator's blood splattered across his face and neck. The small but vociferous crowd inside the arena roared its approval and many got to their feet, baying for more. This is what they had come to see. They wanted to be entertained, but mostly they wanted blood. By the time Corvo had wiped his face with a cloth, Drax, the gladiator who had landed the blow, had already spun round and plunged his gladius into the exposed stomach of the second of his three adversaries. Then, with a snarl of victory, he had viciously twisted his blade before withdrawing it. The wounded man dropped his gladius and shield, and collapsed to his knees, holding his stomach. Wide-eyed, he stared at his slit belly: glistening grey entrails had started to slip out through his fingers, to the delight of the crowd. Raising his head one last time, he made eye contact with Drax. His gaze was met by a pair of cold eyes; there was no remorse or pity there. The stricken gladiator coughed once, dark blood escaping the corners of his mouth, and then he fell face down into the bloodstained sand.

The crowd roared again.

The gladiator whose blood had splattered Corvo was struggling to his feet, his face a ruined mess from where Drax's shield had struck him, shattering his nose and rendering him almost senseless. He had not witnessed his comrade's demise but could now see the lifeless body disgorging its contents onto the arena sand a few paces in front of him. He let out a roar of defiance as he launched himself at Drax's back, but he was too slow, still groggy from the previous blow. In one fluid movement, Drax spun round and slit his throat with the point of his gladius. The thin, red line widened as blood streamed down the man's chest, and he let out a gurgling sound that was lost amongst the excited cheering of the crowd. Then he too collapsed face down in the sand, his blood merging with that of his dead comrade.

Drax struck his shield several times with the pommel of his gladius before raising it high into the air and letting out a mighty roar of his own. The crowd responded in kind, some even chanting Drax's name. He was giving them what they wanted and for today at least, they loved him for it.

Corvo watched attentively as Drax drank in the adulation. *Has the man forgotten there is a third opponent still to be dealt with, or is he so confident that he doesn't care?* he wondered.

The cheers from the crowd started to die down as their attention now turned to the remaining gladiator. There was yet more blood to be had.

Corvo realised that if the last man was to have any chance of defeating Drax, he had to strike now whilst Drax in his arrogance had made himself vulnerable. It wouldn't be an honourable victory, to run the man through from behind, but then Corvo wasn't looking for honourable men necessarily; he was looking for warriors, men prepared to do whatever it took to succeed. Survivors. Killers.

As if picking up on Corvo's thoughts, Drax lowered his gladius and turned to face his remaining opponent. He immediately dropped into a defensive position and raised his shield. The last gladiator was cowering several strides away, showing no inclination to attack. Even from his position in this small, dirty, backstreet stadium, rather ostentatiously named the Mars Gladiatorial Arena, Corvo could see that the man was shaking. Whatever courage he might have once possessed now deserted him, along with the ability to control his bladder. The crowd howled with laughter. Some hurled insults at the gladiator, others rotten fruit. When Drax narrowed his eyes and began to slowly advance upon him, the gladiator began to back further away, drawing the fury of the crowd. They wanted a contest, not an execution.

Drax roared with laughter as he closed in on the man, clearly content that his life was in no danger. He would be able to take his time killing this one, and the crowd would worship him for it.

Seeming to remember he had a slight advantage, the terrified man hefted his spear in his right arm and threw it with all his strength at Drax. It was a poorly aimed throw and Drax was able to divert its flight with his shield, the spear landing harmlessly several strides to his left. Drax continued to close in on the man.

The crowd cheered again — perhaps the gladiator was going to make a contest of it after all. Realising that his advantage had already been squandered, the gladiator whimpered as he struggled to pull out his own gladius. It was obvious to both Corvo and his companion, Optio Lucius Flavius, that this man had probably never held a weapon before today, let alone had any training. It was not going to end well for him.

They watched as the man raised his shield and then took a wild swipe at Drax with his gladius, but Drax merely blocked the stroke with his own shield and then, stooping low, slashed his adversary across his exposed right thigh. The gladiator howled with pain from the deep gash as blood began to run down his leg. The noise from the crowd intensified and Drax revelled in it.

Driven by pain and fear, the gladiator lunged at Drax, but it was an ill-considered attack as the man was already off-balance. Drax quickly turned to one side and his opponent stumbled past him. For good measure, Drax slashed the man across his back before again turning to accept the fleeting adoration of the crowd.

Only Corvo and Flavius didn't cheer.

"It's like watching a lion play with its food," said Flavius.

Corvo nodded his agreement but before he could reply, Drax had already seen off two more desperate attacks, both of which resulted in further wounds for the gladiator. The first one had seen him rewarded with a slash across his unprotected left calf and the next, a deep cut down the right side of his face, which was now covered in blood.

The crowd were by now ecstatic and Corvo could hardly hear himself think, much less take in what Flavius was saying to him. The crowd's joy at another man's suffering disgusted him. It was one thing to watch two equally skilled warriors fight, but when a contest was so imbalanced as to be tantamount to murder, he saw no pleasure in the spectacle.

In the arena Drax adjusted his grip on the gladius as he watched his opponent futilely wipe the blood streaming down his face before readying himself for another attack. Then, as if recognising the hopelessness of his situation, the man threw his shield and gladius to the ground before dropping to his knees.

The crowd howled its displeasure and Drax hesitated. He glanced over at Viccius, his lanista, the man who owned the ludus where he and a number of other gladiators lived and trained. He sat high above the arena, shaded from the merciless afternoon sun, enjoying some dates in the company of other minor Roman dignitaries whilst a slave fanned them. The crowd was baying for blood and after a quick glance around, Viccius nodded to Drax, who strode purposefully behind his opponent and, seizing his long hair, violently yanked his head back, exposing his throat. Then, after glancing once more at his lanista, from whom he received another almost imperceptible nod, he ran his blade across the man's throat before releasing his grip. The dead gladiator fell to the ground. Drax spat on his body and turned to face the crowd.

The noise was deafening and Drax, once a proud warrior of the Chatti tribe of Germania, raised his face and arms to the sky and absorbed the adulation. Behind him slaves were already dragging the dead bodies from the arena, whilst others collected the weapons and covered the blood with fresh sand. The cheers from the crowd died down as they talked animatedly amongst themselves and waited for the next contest. With one last look at the small crowd seated around the now clean and restored arena, Drax headed for the tunnel, his departure barely noticed or acknowledged.

"I've seen enough. Let's go," said Corvo, getting to his feet and turning to leave.

"There are several more contests yet. Are you sure you don't want to stay and watch them? Someone else might catch your eye," replied Flavius.

"If, as I suspect, the rest of them are of the same quality as Drax's opponents, then they will be of no use to us. These are not gladiators, but criminals and debtors being offered up as sacrifices for entertainment. Besides, I can't endure this stench much longer."

"The great unwashed of Rome's underbelly mixed with the unmistakeable smell of blood and death. Makes you proud to be Roman, does it not?" said Flavius, grinning.

Corvo didn't respond and was attempting to wipe the last of the blood from his face as he made his way past the people sitting in the front row towards the steps leading to the exit. Annoyed by him pushing past them, some threw insults and threats. One scowl from Corvo was enough to silence them. Content that most of the blood had been removed, Corvo placed the bloody rag over his face and tried to protect his nose from the offending stench.

"I told you we should have gone to one of the better arenas," complained Flavius as he followed his friend.

"Do I need to remind you, Lucius, that what we are to undertake is to be kept secret? If we attempted to recruit men from the more well-known arenas, questions would be asked, and our patron's identity could be at risk. That would have unfavourable repercussions for us all."

"I'm not sure that the lowlifes who frequent these places can be trusted to keep their mouths shut either, Marcus," replied Flavius, glancing around.

"That's why I don't intend on telling them the truth and why you're about to become somebody different." Flavius raised a questioning eyebrow, but didn't press his friend. "Now come, let us go and seal this business and leave this place." Corvo started to make his way up the wooden steps towards the top of the stand from where another set of steps led down to the street. All around them the cheers of the crowd began to erupt as the next set of gladiators were led out onto the sand and introduced.

More lambs for the slaughter, thought Corvo as he began to descend the steps towards the street.

Shortly afterwards, the two soldiers who were dressed in civilian attire stood outside the arena waiting for Viccius to emerge. Corvo had earlier paid a slave to pass a message to him that he would be grateful for a few moments of his time. In truth, Corvo couldn't think of anything he wanted to do less; the man profited from other people's misery. He was not the sort of acquaintance Corvo would normally seek out, but in this instance the needs of the mission had to come first.

As they awaited Viccius' arrival, Corvo glanced around. Outside the arena were a number of barred cages on carts, inside of which were bloodied and wounded gladiators, watched over by bored-looking guards. The gladiators stared out at the two Romans with a mix of emotions. Hate was prevalent, but many of the men's faces showed only relief — relief at having survived to fight another day. Another, larger cart to their left was stacked with the bodies of dead gladiators, some whole, some missing limbs. The pile was getting higher by the minute as an almost constant stream of slaves brought more bodies out from under the arena. Corvo recognised the body of the gladiator whose blood had splattered his face. It was a grisly sight and Corvo had no wish to tarry, as the heat and blood had started to attract flies by the score.

"Is this him?" asked Flavius when he saw an overweight man with thinning hair emerge from the arena tunnel. He was attended by three slaves, one a huge man in his late twenties who was obviously one of his gladiators assigned bodyguard duty, a smaller, wiry man of roughly the same age as his master, and the slave whom Corvo had paid to pass on his request for a meeting. This slave pointed at Corvo and Flavius and then hurried away. Employing as much dignity as he could muster, the lanista slowly made his way over to Corvo and Flavius.

"It is. Let me do the talking," said Corvo.

"As you wish."

The lanista stopped in front of them. "Greetings, citizens. I am Tiberius Lucus Viccius, lanista of the Ludus Viccius, the greatest ludus this side of the Tiber. I understand you wish to speak with me?"

"Greetings, Viccius. I am Luculus and this is my associate, Ventelus," said Corvo, using their assumed names. "We are here on behalf of a third party who is interested in purchasing one of your gladiators."

"Are you now?" Viccius eyed them suspiciously. "And who is it you're interested in purchasing, and why? I've never seen you before."

"Drax, and our reasons are our own," replied Corvo.

"I see. Well, if you watched him fight you will realise that he is one of my prize assets and I am loath to let him go," said Viccius, smiling, though the smile never quite reached his eyes.

"Come now, Viccius, everyone has their price. Name yours," prompted Corvo.

Viccius made a great show of sucking air in through his teeth. He turned and had a whispered exchange with the elder slave before smiling again at Corvo. "Fifty denarii."

"That is robbery. I doubt your whole ludus is worth that," exclaimed Flavius indignantly.

"Then we are done here, and I'll bid you a good day," said Viccius, making to leave.

Corvo gave his friend a withering look and then smiled back at Viccius. "Ten denarii."

"Ten? You insult me, friend. Forty denarii and no less."

"Fifteen."

"Thirty, or I walk away now." Without being instructed to, the larger of the two slaves took a step nearer, as if to emphasise his master's point.

Corvo was unfazed. "Twenty and no little bird chirps in the emperor's ear about how you are not paying all your taxes or how you cover his bust up when nobody is visiting your villa," said Corvo. He was no longer smiling.

Viccius paled. "Who are you?" he asked, narrowing his eyes.

"Just an agent acting for a third party who wants to buy one of your gladiators for a fair price and with no questions asked," replied Corvo.

"But why Drax? I have better prospects than him. He'd as soon cut your throat as fight for you."

"Then it sounds like we would be doing you a favour taking him off your hands and that my last offer of twenty denarii was too generous. Still, I'm prepared to honour it. Do we have a bargain or not?"

Viccius looked at Corvo then clasped his arm to confirm the deal. "Twenty denarii?"

Corvo nodded and dropped a small brown pouch into Viccius' palm. Viccius hefted its weight and, seemingly satisfied, instructed the older slave to arrange for Drax to be brought to him.

After a brief wait, Drax was led out of the tunnel, flanked by two guards who warily remained a couple of paces behind him. Drax was now just in a loincloth, having been divested of his armour and weapons the moment he departed the arena.

"Drax, these men … Luculus and Ventelus, are your new masters," said Viccius, matter-of-factly.

Drax looked shocked. "You have sold me, Dominus?" he asked in faltering Latin.

"I have."

"But did I not please you? I won. It was not my fault the contest was so short and my opponents so poor. I will try and put on more of a show next time."

"You have served me well, Drax, but your star is waning. It is time for new blood in Ludus Viccius. Go now, and may good fortune be upon you." And with that Viccius nodded to Corvo and Flavius before turning and walking away. After a few paces he stopped, turned, and faced Corvo. "Who was it who told you about the emperor's bust? Was it Flacchus?"

"I can't tell you, but I advise you to be more careful in the future."

"It *was* Flacchus. I knew it." He stormed off, muttering to himself.

"Who is Flacchus?" Flavius asked.

"I've no idea," replied Corvo.

"So who did tell you about the emperor's bust?"

"The same slave who passed him our message told me about it for a couple of coins."

"But what if the slave had lied?"

"Wouldn't matter. Viccius' fate would be the same should the emperor ever hear."

"And the taxes?"

"Few pay all the tax they're obliged to, so the odds on that being true of Viccius were always in my favour."

Flavius shook his head in amusement.

Drax had been listening to their exchange as he watched Viccius recede into the distance and now turned to the two Romans and eyed them suspiciously. "So, I am to be your gladiator now, I take it?"

Corvo didn't immediately reply. He was irked by the tone of the slave but didn't want the first words he said to the man to be a reprimand. "No, if you do as I say, your days as a gladiator are over. However, I do have need of your skills with a sword."

"I am to be an assassin then?"

"Not an assassin. Come, let us find somewhere to get a drink," said Corvo, mopping his brow and casting an accusatory glance at the sun, "and we will tell you of our plans."

"And if I don't like them?"

"I'm not at all interested in whether you like them, Drax, just that you obey me."

"And what's to stop me from just taking your drink and then running? There are only two of you and neither of you appear armed, though I suspect you have daggers hidden in the folds of your togas."

"Oh, we're not alone, Drax. There are others hidden in the shadows, watching us as we speak, and I can assure you they are armed and very capable. Now, are you coming to hear what I have to say, or do you want to put what I have just told you to the test?"

As a demonstration of his confidence, Corvo gestured for Flavius to follow and then turned his back on Drax and started to make his way to the Wild Boar tavern they had passed on the way to the arena.

CHAPTER 2

"I'd heard you Romans were stretched thin guarding your borders, but I didn't realise you were so desperate for soldiers that you were recruiting men like me." Drax laughed as he took another mouthful of wine. "And who else is in this company?"

"We have some veterans, some serving soldiers, some other gladiators and a few men we've … borrowed from gaol," said Flavius.

"That doesn't inspire me."

"You don't need to be inspired, Drax. You just need to follow orders and do your job," snapped Corvo. He glanced around, checking that nobody was listening to their conversation.

"And what exactly is my job?"

"Killing people… It's what you're good at, isn't it? Though the men we are likely to be fighting will provide you with more of a challenge than those unfortunates you faced earlier."

"I can only kill who they put in front of me," said Drax with a shrug. "I should be fighting real warriors in the big arenas, not cowards in back-alley slums."

"Well, if this goes well, your days of fighting in any arena will be over and you'll be a free man again."

Raised voices at the back of the tavern drew their attention. Moments later a brawl broke out between two groups of about a dozen men. Drax started to rise, but a restraining hand and a shake of the head from Corvo saw him reluctantly resume his seat.

"Not your fight, Drax."

Corvo watched from his seat as the brawl escalated. All the men looked well-fed and fit, and Corvo had no doubt that he was watching a fight between soldiers representing two different legions, or even different cohorts of the same legion — an all too frequent occurrence, particularly in the seedier taverns of Rome's backstreets. Wine, pride and honour were a potent and often deadly mix.

Corvo winced as a burly man with a shaved head grabbed an adversary around the neck before ramming his head into a wooden pillar. Blood started to pour from a huge gash on his forehead and he stumbled to the floor, knocking a small table over in the process. His assailant was immediately hit over the head with a stool, causing him to stumble but not fall, a testament to the man's strength and ability to take pain.

"He could be a handy man to have around," commented Flavius as he quickly leant forward to avoid being struck by another man who had just been hurled across the floor in their direction. Apart from them and those fighting, the tavern was fast emptying, nobody wanting to be inadvertently dragged into the melee.

"Agreed," replied Corvo. "Time to break this up, I think."

"And just how are you going to do that? They're never going to listen to you. You're not in uniform, remember."

"I've got to try…" Before Corvo could attempt anything, the tavern door burst open, and a man known to at least some of the combatants hurried in.

"The Urban Cohorts are coming."

The majority of the fighting immediately ceased, although one man took the opportunity to punch the man standing to his left, and all the fighters quickly departed. The man whose head had been rammed into the wooden pillar was unable to stand unaided and he had to be helped out by two of his comrades. Soon, broken furniture and blood splatters on the floor and up the walls were the only evidence that an altercation had taken place. Less than a minute later the sound of many pairs of hobnail shoes running past reached their ears as the Urban Cohorts half-heartedly gave chase.

"Time for us to leave too," said Corvo, draining his mug. "Pity the Urban Cohorts came; it's denied me the chance to speak to that big man with the shaved head."

When Flavius didn't immediately respond Corvo followed his friend's gaze, which was fixed on a stout-looking middle-aged man sitting in the far corner. Although he had the unmistakeable bearing of a military man, he had not taken part in the skirmish. "What is it, Lucius?"

"It can't be."

"Lucius?"

"Forgive me, Marcus, I just need a minute to check something. If I'm right, you needn't worry about missing out on that brute a minute ago."

"I thought his name was Ventelus, not Lucius?" said a confused-looking Drax as he snatched Flavius' cup and swallowed the dribble of wine left inside it. "Come to that, I thought your name was Luculus?"

"I'll explain later," said Corvo irritably as he watched his friend cross the floor and sit in front of the stranger. They spoke briefly, though they were too far away for Corvo to hear what they said, and then Flavius pointed at Corvo and Drax and beckoned for the other man to follow him. The older man rose slowly and downed his drink before confidently striding over to where Corvo and Drax were sitting.

"Marcus, this is Centurion Titus Galba of the Sixth. Titus, this is Centurion Marcus Ovidius Corvo and Drax, a … former gladiator." A strange look crossed Galba's face at the mention of Corvo's name. "Marcus, Titus would be worth his weight in silver to our mission. Titus, please take a seat. I think you're going to like what Marcus has to say."

Galba raised an eyebrow and after clasping arms with Corvo but pointedly ignoring Drax, he took a seat, whilst Flavius signalled for more wine to be brought over to their table.

"Corvo," said Galba, eyeing his fellow centurion as he mulled the name over. "You wouldn't happen to be related to Maximus Corvo, would you?"

"He was my grandfather."

"Your grandfather was the man who died protecting an eagle when Varus' legions were wiped out in the forests by that traitor Arminius?"

Corvo nodded.

"He was a true hero of Rome," said Galba with great respect.

"So they say."

"And your father died in much the same way, as I recall?"

"He did. Putting down a revolt in Mauretania some years later."

"You must be very proud."

"I am."

"It's a lot to have to live up to."

"I do what I can."

"My father spoke fondly of Maximus. He wasn't there in the forest that day, but he had served with him before, when he was just a raw recruit and your grandfather was one of the old sweats. Probably knew your father too." Galba took a gulp of his wine and wiped his mouth with the back of his hand before eyeing the three men suspiciously. "So let me get this straight. From what I understand from my nephew here..."

"Your what?" interrupted Corvo in surprise.

"Nephew," repeated Galba, slightly irritated.

"Titus is my mother's brother," said Flavius by way of explanation.

"I see," said Corvo, raising an eyebrow before gesturing for Galba to continue.

"As I was saying, Lucius was just explaining how you have a proposition that may interest me. Something about me accompanying you on a highly dangerous mission, one that you can't tell me about yet, in the company of a woefully inadequate force comprised of some of the worst scum in the Empire?" He glanced at Drax before continuing. "The pay is pitiful, and should we run into trouble, which by the sound of it we almost certainly will, we'll be on our own with no hope of support? Does that sum it up, do you think?"

"Optio Flavius really shouldn't have gone discussing such things with strangers without my prior approval," said Corvo, glaring at his friend who at least had the good sense to look sheepish. "But yes, that sums it up."

"You left out the part about travelling the world and meeting new friends," said Flavius, grinning. "And Titus isn't a stranger, not to me, at least."

"And when did you last see Centurion Galba, Lucius?" Corvo demanded, noting that the sheepish look was back. "If you have not seen him recently, then to all intents and purposes he is a stranger, and I would caution you to not go discussing our mission with anyone else without first speaking to me. Understood?"

Flavius nodded his understanding.

Galba stared at the two friends and then burst into laughter. "You're both mad… When do I start?"

"Our patron will arrange for your temporary release from the Sixth, though I thought the Sixth were currently in Egypt?"

said Corvo. "So, you can join us whenever you've tidied up any unfinished business you might have."

"The Sixth are in Egypt, but I was seconded to … administrative duties here in Rome. As for unfinished business…" He reached for his cup and downed the last of his wine. "Done. Let's go."

"Is the reason for your secondment anything for me to worry about?" asked Corvo.

"You? No. Others? Yes." Galba stood up and headed for the door.

After exchanging a glance, Corvo and Flavius followed him out into the late afternoon sunshine, where he was squinting. Evidently, he had been in the gloom of the tavern for some time, though to Corvo's surprise he didn't appear at all drunk. He was either a slow drinker or held his wine extremely well. A moment later Drax too emerged into the sunlight, muttering about there still being plenty of wine to drink.

"Stay where you are! I want a word with you four!" roared a voice.

Corvo turned to see nine men in the uniform of the Urban Cohort. Their leader took a step forward. "I understand you were involved in the altercation inside this tavern earlier." It was a statement, not a question. "You're coming with us. You can either come quietly, or, if you prefer —" he slapped his cosh into his palm menacingly — "the hard way. It's up to you."

"My name is —" began Corvo.

"I don't give a rat's arse what your name is. If you disturb the peace on my watch, you're going to answer for it."

"You're making a mistake —"

"No, you're the one making the mistake, testing my patience."

"Look —"

"Suit yourself, the hard way it is. Boys," he addressed the men behind him.

Until this point Galba had kept his back to the Urban Cohort men, but now he slowly turned to face them, drawing himself up to his full height as he did so. For a Roman, Galba was tall and coupled with his bulk, he made an impressive figure.

The leader licked his lips, his eyes fixed on Galba as he took a couple of paces backwards.

"It seems I was mistaken; you're not the men we are looking for. Be on your way." Despite his bravado, Corvo could see the man was petrified.

Corvo glared at the man as he pointedly pushed his way through the Cohort men, Flavius and Drax at his side. A couple of moments later Galba followed, but this time the Cohort men moved aside, allowing him to pass unhindered.

"What was all that about?" Corvo asked Flavius as they strode down the cobbled street.

"My uncle has a reputation for being able to look after himself. I'm surprised the leader didn't recognise him."

"When we get a chance, you must tell me why it is we've allowed Galba to join our mission."

"Trust me, Marcus, you won't regret it."

"I'll hold you to that, my friend."

Behind them, Galba was drunkenly singing some old bawdy marching song as he followed them. The wine had apparently got to him after all.

They had walked a short distance further before Galba staggered up alongside the others, throwing an arm around Flavius' shoulder as if for support. "We're being followed," he announced, perfectly coherently.

"Who by, the Cohort?" asked Corvo, turning to face Galba. His drunkenness had evidently been an act.

"I don't know. One man — he's dressed like an ordinary citizen but moves like he's got some sort of military training. He's been following us ever since the tavern. Keep walking or he'll know we're onto him."

"He was in the tavern?" asked Corvo.

"No, he was skulking in the shadows outside," said Drax, joining the discussion. "I noticed him watching the confrontation from an alley."

"We need to find out who he is and what he wants," said Corvo. While he spoke, he was looking over the other men's shoulders, trying to see who was following them, but nobody stood out. The man was either very good or Corvo was very bad at identifying pursuers.

"There's an alley just up here on the left. You three carry on and I'll pretend that I'm going down there to piss. When he passes, I'll double back and come up behind him," suggested Galba.

"And what if it's you he's after?" asked Flavius. "You no doubt have your share of enemies, Uncle."

Galba grinned. "I do and if it is, it won't end well for him."

"I would prefer to take the man alive and find out why he's following us," interjected Corvo. "If our mission is compromised, I need to know how and whether others may be following us."

"I'll do my best, but no promises," said Galba.

For a moment Corvo thought he saw a man peering at them from within a passing crowd, but when he looked again, the man had vanished.

"All right, let's do it."

Singing another raucous marching song, Galba made a great show of stumbling down the alley as the others carried on. Peeking over his shoulder, Corvo noticed a man stride past, casting a very quick glance down the alley.

The man increased his pace and was now no more than ten paces behind Corvo. When their pursuer was almost upon them, Corvo spun round and saw Galba had caught up with them. Corvo extended his dagger towards the stranger's throat, but he was quicker, and from beneath his cloak he withdrew two gladii. The tip of one pressed against Corvo's throat, and the other extended backwards, pressed against Galba's chest. How the man had reacted so quickly was a mystery to Corvo.

"I had hoped to break words in a more civilised manner," said the stranger, grinning at Corvo.

"Then why didn't you? You've been watching and following us for some time," said Corvo.

"True, but I didn't want to run afoul of the Urban Cohort."

"Who are you and what do you want?"

"I can't make up my mind whether I should feel insulted that you don't recognise me. Still, no matter. I am Atilus."

"Atilus?" queried Corvo.

"Gladiator," said Drax.

"No more. Now I am a free man. I won my freedom."

"They finally grew tired of watching you kill old men, did they?" sneered Drax.

Atilus kept the points of his weapons in place but turned his gaze on Drax. "You think yourself a gladiator, but you're no better than a rabid dog fighting in the pits for scraps. You wouldn't have lasted two heartbeats with even the lowest of the men in my ludus, or any other for that matter. No one will remember your name."

"Why don't you give me one of your gladii and we'll see about that right now, you and I?" snarled Drax.

"Now is not the time, Drax," said Corvo. "What is it you want, Atilus?"

Quick as a flash, Atilus removed his gladii and then concealed them beneath his cloak once more. "I hear you are recruiting men for some mission. I find myself between jobs and would like to volunteer."

"Who told you that?" asked Corvo, massaging his throat where the sword point had been held.

"I hear things in the brothels and taverns."

"Not this."

"Yet still I know."

"So it seems. And you wish to accompany us without knowing what the mission is? Is there another reason you are so willing to join us, Atilus, other than your unemployment, I mean?"

Atilus smiled. "Did I not mention that I also find myself light of coin at an unfortunate time?"

"And by unfortunate, you mean…?"

"I may owe a powerful and unforgiving man from the Serpentine some money, a lot of money, and it would probably be wise if I left the city for a while."

"A failed gladiator and a debtor," smirked Drax.

"Silence!" barked Corvo, tiring of the sniping. "And apart from your obvious skills with a sword, what would you bring to our group, Atilus?"

"Well, I know how to track someone and can organise a better trap than any of you, it seems."

"We knew you were following us," said Flavius.

"You stuck out like a Vestal Virgin at an orgy," added Drax dismissively. "I saw you following us from the Wild Boar."

"Oh, I've been following you two for far longer than that," replied Atilus, looking at Corvo and Flavius. "And as for your trap, I've seen the big man —" he nodded at Galba — "quaff a lot of wine before and it never seems to affect him, so I wasn't buying the whole drunk as a senator routine when he went down the alley. I knew he'd be coming up behind me soon after."

"I said I should have gone," said Drax.

"I'm not letting you out of my sight just yet," replied Corvo.

"You don't trust me?"

"No, I don't trust you, Drax."

"Whatever you decide, Marcus, do it quickly. We're attracting a lot of attention, standing here and waving swords at one another," said Flavius. "Swords we're not allowed to carry within city limits, remember?"

Corvo glanced around and saw that they were indeed the subject of many people's conversations. They needed to move, to get off the streets. "Join us then, Atilus. I can always use another sword, but you might not thank me when you learn our mission and likely fate."

"Don't concern yourself … Marcus. Fate is my friend, fickle though she may be."

After a last glance around, Corvo gestured for the others to follow him as they tried to make an inconspicuous exit.

CHAPTER 3

Leaving Flavius in charge of the small but growing band of men, early the next morning Corvo and Galba headed for the quarry at Mida. Corvo had been intending to take Flavius with him as his most trusted friend, but had changed his mind at the last minute, deciding the ride would give him the opportunity to get to know the big centurion and whether he was going to have an issue with taking orders from someone much younger and less experienced than himself. Galba would also be a deterrent to anyone who intended Corvo harm, and there was always the chance that he might know some of the men they were heading to see.

Corvo had left instructions with Flavius to prepare the buildings they had been loaned to accommodate up to sixty men. He was also to secure enough provisions to see them to the coast and across the sea. From there on they would have to buy provisions where they could, and steal them where they couldn't.

"You know that these men are cowards, Centurion?" said Galba after a long silence. When they had first left, both men had wanted to take the opportunity to learn about the other, but once their curiosity had been sated, conversation had dried up.

"I know what they're accused of, but I wasn't there, so I can't say with any certainty that they are what people say they are."

"That's very charitable of you, Centurion, if not a little naive. These men are everything they say and more. They refused to advance and press home the attack. Many decent men lost their lives that day because of their cowardice. They should have been decimated or crucified, not sent to a quarry. Why should they still be allowed to draw breath when braver men no longer can because of their cowardice?"

"You know them?" asked Corvo, turning in his saddle to look at Galba.

"I was there that day … in Germania. I watched as they disobeyed their orders and refused to help their comrades … their brothers. I had to watch helplessly as brave men, some of them my friends, were slaughtered whilst these miserable wretches stood trembling behind their shields like frightened old women."

"And the fact that your legion is now in Egypt, and you're not, is somehow tied up in all this, isn't it?"

"There was trouble in camp when the battle was eventually won, no thanks to them. Men were angry, vengeful, and rightly so. A fight erupted and … well, let's just say the man who instigated their mutiny is no longer with us."

"You killed him?"

"Not intentionally, but yes. Most of the leaders of the mutiny were executed, but not all of them. One of them still draws breath and was sent here with the rank and file who took part. The quarry at Mida may well be Hades, but it still isn't enough for what he and his comrades did."

"And your punishment was to be sent to Rome on administrative duties?"

Galba snorted in derision. "At one stage it looked like I too might be executed or sent to Mida, but threads were pulled, my long service was taken into account, and instead, yes, I was seconded to 'administrative work'. It would have been better to kill me quickly than make me suffer that slow death."

Corvo smiled; he could only imagine how frustrating Galba had found his new role. "So how many of the men sentenced to the quarry do you know?"

"By name, just the one I mentioned, Caeso Traianus. Nasty piece of work. How he escaped execution baffles me. I'd probably recognise some of the others, though. Not the type of men you want to forget, much less have standing in a battle formation at your side."

"Unfortunately, Titus, given the nature of the mission we are to undertake, the only men available to me, save for the handful of regulars like yourself, are the dregs of the Empire. Men the Empire would consider expendable, if she even knew about the mission. Men like Traianus."

"Hmm. Perhaps not the wisest idea."

"Probably not, but that's the job," said Corvo. "Still want to come?" Before Galba could answer, Corvo suddenly reined in and held up his hand. "Do you hear that?"

"It's the men working the quarry, just over that ridge," said Galba, pointing.

"We're here already? We've made good time, it seems," said Corvo, taking a mouthful of water. The sun was beating down and despite not being dressed in uniform or armour, it was still uncomfortably hot. He offered the water to Galba, but he shook his head.

"Centurion, watch yourself here. These are desperate men who have given up hope and would do anything to escape this life."

"Thank you, Titus, but I'm sure I'll be fine. The guards will be alert for trouble."

"It is the guards of which I speak. They are just as much prisoners here as the men they oversee. Failed soldiers not fit for anything else, each carrying a grudge."

Corvo considered the warning and then nodded his acknowledgement. "Then let's make this as brief as possible, and I trust you to watch my back." With that he nudged his horse and resumed the journey.

If there was a Tartarus, or a Hades or whatever the Underworld was truly called, Corvo was sure he was looking at it now. He thought they'd been hot approaching the ridge overlooking the quarry, but once they had started to carefully descend the narrow winding track into the quarry itself, the temperature had increased considerably. All around them were hundreds of men, some bare-chested, some in rags, hammering away at rocks or the base of the valley with rudimentary tools. Others were seemingly tasked with carrying the rocks to waiting carts, all of them watched over by a score of surly-looking guards.

Every now and then Corvo would hear the tell-tale crack of a whip as a man was lashed for some transgression, real or imagined. At least two men lay motionless in the dust, having either collapsed from heat exhaustion or perhaps hunger. No attempt had been made to remove their bodies. To his left as he arrived at the basin of the quarry, three more men were tied to posts, completely exposed to the scorching sun. Their backs were a livid mess of red welts and open cuts where the lash had been diligently employed. Most of the workers looked emaciated, though some were in better shape, presumably either having only just arrived or perhaps as a result of stealing other men's food. Corvo imagined it was very much a case of dog eat dog here.

An overweight man in a uniform made up of bits of legionary kit that probably used to fit him came striding up to Corvo, flanked by four men attired in much the same way. Two of them grabbed the reins of Corvo's and Galba's horses.

Galba grunted and the man holding his reins stepped back without letting go..

"State your name and your business here," demanded the overweight man who Corvo took to be their commander.

"My name is Luculus, and this is my friend Ventelus. My business is only for the ears of whoever commands here."

"That would be me, Nonus Seneca."

"Well then, Seneca, where can we go to talk?"

"I'm not sure we have anything to discuss."

"Is that so? That's a pity." Corvo reached into his saddlebag and withdrew a pouch that was clearly full of coins. He hefted it in his hand to demonstrate its weight. "Then I have clearly wasted my time and will take my business elsewhere."

Seneca's eyes widened at the sight of the coin bag. "What's to stop me from just taking the money and killing you both?"

"There's nothing to stop you from trying, of course, but I wouldn't consider it your wisest decision today," replied Corvo.

Galba placed his hand on the hilt of his gladius and glared at the men standing around the commander.

"You are but two. We are over twenty. You'd stand no chance," ventured Seneca, grinning like a man who believed he had the upper hand.

"Perhaps, but how long do you think these men will stay acquiescent once they see an opportunity to escape?" Corvo gestured towards the prisoners, some of whom had risked the lash by stopping work to observe the exchange. "I would imagine that most have reason to hate you and your men. Given the chance, I doubt their revenge will be swift and merciful, so I suggest you consider your next words very carefully."

Seneca's men had begun to fidget and glance about. Corvo's words had apparently rung true.

"Very well, I will grant you a brief audience, but I caution you to not waste my time. Follow me." The man turned and headed towards a small stone building with a well outside.

"See that our horses are watered and nothing is taken, or I will hold you personally responsible," Galba instructed the man holding his reins. He climbed down and strode after Corvo.

"So what is it you want, Luculus?" asked Seneca, lowering his bulk onto a wooden stool and gesturing for his guests to sit. Corvo sat but Galba remained standing with his back against the wall. One of Seneca's men had also remained in the room and now stood blocking the exit.

"Perhaps we could talk alone?" suggested Corvo, gesturing towards the guard.

"Anything you have to say to me you can say in front of Spurius."

"As you wish. I want to buy the release of twenty-five men, including Caeso Traianus."

Seneca stared at Corvo and then burst out laughing. He was soon joined by Spurius. Neither Corvo nor Galba joined in, although Corvo did allow himself a small smile.

"This is a work camp. You cannot just buy men," said Seneca.

"And why is that? Because you're so diligent about your duties?" asked Corvo caustically.

Seneca's expression turned dark. "Because I said so."

"Are you sure about that?" asked Corvo, hefting the pouch again.

"Why do you want them, and why Traianus in particular?" asked Seneca, his eyes trained on the pouch.

"My patron has stated that a condition of this deal would be that no questions are asked, nor do you speak of it to anyone outside this quarry. Further, if the men prove useful, my patron will likely require more men, many more, at some point in the future. This could become quite lucrative for you, Seneca, and anyone else you care to involve. But we'd need men, not walking corpses. I would suggest that if you agree to this deal, you start feeding the prisoners."

"Interesting. But what of my work here, supplying the raw materials the Empire needs? Who will help me achieve my quotas?"

"You're a clever man, Seneca. I'm sure you'll think of something. One thing the Empire is never short of is slaves and prisoners. So, do we have a deal?" Corvo extended his arm.

Seneca clasped arms with him, and the bargain was struck.

"I shall be glad to be rid of Traianus; the man is nothing but trouble. Spurius, have Traianus and twenty-four other men lined up outside as soon as possible. In the meantime, our new business partners and I will share a cup of wine."

Spurius nodded curtly and went outside to carry out his orders, leaving the others to toast the deal.

A short while later Corvo, Galba and Seneca emerged into the bright sunshine to find twenty-five men lined up waiting for them.

"There, Traianus and twenty-four men as requested. I'll have that pouch now," said Seneca, holding out his palm.

Corvo rounded on the man, making Seneca flinch and Galba reach for his gladius. "You think you can cheat me, Seneca? You take me for a fool? I wanted men, not corpses."

"They are all like this. That's what hard labour and small rations do to a man. It's nothing less than they deserve."

"Maybe, yet *he* looks fit and healthy by comparison," said Corvo, pointing at Traianus. He had never met Traianus, but he instinctively knew that the one man who looked as if he wasn't hours away from death was him. "You are Traianus?"

The man nodded and held Corvo's gaze.

"Some are better suited to the conditions. He is an isolated case," said Seneca dismissively.

"I doubt that. I can see we have wasted each other's time here. We'll be on our way."

"By all means leave, but we struck a bargain, so you'll be leaving the pouch when you go." Seneca gently flicked his head and immediately Spurius and two other guards rushed towards Galba.

By the time Corvo had drawn his own gladius and turned, one man had been run through and another lay on the dusty ground, clutching a gaping wound in his throat out of which bright red blood now pumped. Spurius found himself disarmed with Galba's left arm wrapped around his neck and the bloody gladius pressed hard against his side.

A ghastly gurgling sound emanated from the man whose throat had been slit and then he breathed no more.

"Your move, Seneca," said Corvo as another three guards warily approached them. He had been astounded by the speed with which Galba had dealt with his three adversaries.

Seneca waved for his men to back off and sheathe their weapons. "Come, come, this is nothing but a misunderstanding. How can we reinvigorate this deal?"

"Take the shackles off Traianus and let him select twenty-four other men," Corvo demanded.

"Are you mad? I'll not remove his shackles; he's just as likely to kill me."

"You will if you want this deal to go ahead, otherwise my angry friend here might kill you. And the men Traianus selects are all to have their shackles removed too."

"Then it won't just be me who dies at his hand — freeing that many men will ensure both of you will join me in the afterlife."

"Get on with it, Seneca. My patience grows thin."

Seneca signalled for a guard to release Traianus, which he reluctantly did, hurrying away from the man as soon as he could.

"Traianus, I want you to pick twenty-four of your best men, men who can fight and aren't going to drop dead on me over the next few days. No questions now, just do it. Do you understand?" asked Corvo. Traianus narrowed his eyes at Corvo and then curtly nodded. "Then go and do it and bring them back here, where they will be unshackled."

Shortly after, Traianus returned with a cluster of shackled men trailing after him. Without being ordered, they formed a rough line behind Traianus. They were hardly the strongest and fittest men Corvo had ever seen, but better than those that Seneca had tried to foist on him. They were fit enough — the hard labour would have seen to that. They just needed some decent rations and proper sleep to enable them to get their strength back.

Corvo slowly marched along the line, staring into each man's eyes. Somewhere deep inside each, the heart of a legionary still burned. He wondered if they regretted their mutiny and would jump at the chance to redeem themselves, or whether they would stab him in the back the first chance they got.

"Unshackle them."

Seneca nodded to two of his men and they quickly went along the line, releasing the prisoners. Corvo noticed that the rest of Seneca's guards grasped their weapons in readiness for trouble. The whole quarry had ground to a halt in anticipation.

"Prisoners, today is your lucky day, because I am about to take you away from this pit of misery."

There were some muted cheers, mostly from the younger men. The old ones knew there would be a catch — there always was.

"Soldiers you once were, and soldiers you will again be." This provoked more interest. "We will take you to a barracks just outside Rome. It's not quite a senator's villa on Sardinia, but I suspect compared to your current accommodation it may feel so."

This drew some genuine laughter, although the undercurrent of suspicion continued.

"There you will be given a few days' rest and some decent food. Once you have regained your strength, you will join me on a mission where you will no doubt have the opportunity to regain your honour."

"What is this mission of which you speak?" asked one of the men.

"All will be revealed in due course. Suffice to say it will be more mentally stimulating than your current employment." More laughter, louder this time. He was winning them over. He glanced at Traianus, whose expression remained impassive.

"And what if we don't want to go on this mission?" asked the same man.

"Then you are more than welcome to remain here. I'm sure Seneca will keep your bunk free."

"And what's to stop us just running away once we leave this place? We are unshackled and there are only two of you, unless you have a legion hidden over that ridge."

"There is no legion hidden over the ridge or anywhere else for that matter. So yes, you can run if you so desire, but I rather suspect you might end up like these men who were foolish enough to cross my large friend over there." Corvo gestured towards the two dead guards and Galba. It was only then that Corvo realised that Galba was still holding Spurius around the neck with a sword to his side. "You can let him go now, Ventelus."

With a hard shove, Spurius went stumbling forward. Once he'd regained his feet, he glared at Galba.

Corvo noticed a strange look cross Traianus' face as he stared at Galba, and he wondered if it was a flicker of recognition. Galba was not the type of man you could easily forget.

"Now, those of you who wish to join us, take one pace forward." As one, every man stepped forward so that they were level with Traianus. "And what say you, Traianus? Will you join us and seek to regain your honour?"

After a short pause, Traianus stepped forward, so he was once again in front of his men. He stared at Galba, and Corvo was certain that Traianus had recognised the big centurion even though he had referred to him as Ventelus.

"Then our business here is done." Corvo turned and threw the pouch to Seneca, who nimbly caught it. As Corvo had hoped, every guard and prisoner had witnessed the transaction and were now watching Seneca with covetous eyes.

Good, thought Corvo, *that should give him some problems.* "All right, we've a long march back to barracks, where I'm told a hot meal will be awaiting you." The men all cheered. "Ventelus, the wineskins."

Galba turned and untied a number of empty wineskins attached to his saddle and threw them on the ground. "Drink your fill and then fill these up, then we'll be on our way."

Corvo climbed back onto his horse as the men rushed to the well and drank greedily, much to the watchful annoyance of Seneca and the envy of the prisoners being left behind. When everybody was satiated and the wineskins full, the men fell into step behind Corvo.

There was suddenly a roar of anger, and Corvo turned in his saddle to see Traianus threateningly close to Galba and Spurius rushing towards the pair of them, his sword raised. It looked to Corvo as if Traianus was reaching for Galba's gladius, ready to strike him down, and Spurius had seen the danger and was rushing to intervene.

The next few moments proved Corvo wrong. Traianus was indeed reaching for Galba's gladius, but as soon as he had snatched it from the centurion's belt he spun round to attack Spurius. In one fluid movement, Traianus brought his weapon up in an arc, deflecting Spurius' sword arm and disarming him, before switching his grip and driving the gladius into Spurius' midriff with a powerful back thrust. Traianus thrust the blade all the way in and stared into the other man's eyes as the light in them gradually faded.

"That's for my men you've killed." He withdrew the blade.

Spurius issued a muffled grunt before his lifeless body crumpled to the ground. Traianus' men cheered whilst Seneca and his remaining guards looked on, fear etched on their faces.

"My weapon," said Galba, holding out his hand.

Traianus handed it over, handle first.

"My thanks."

Traianus nodded as the two men locked eyes but said nothing to indicate that he recognised Galba.

Corvo turned back in his saddle and gestured for everyone to follow.

Mindful of their physical state, Corvo led them at a gentle pace up the narrow winding path and over the ridge until they were on flat, open ground. Free of their shackles and the lash for the first time in many weeks, the men seemed in remarkably good spirits as Corvo encouraged them along. They had only gone a couple of miles when someone shouted a warning that a rider was approaching from behind.

Corvo turned and shielded his eyes. "Anyone recognise him?"

"Looks like one of the guards from the quarry," said one of Traianus' men.

Corvo looked to Traianus for confirmation. He nodded.

The rider soon reined in next to Corvo and removed the scarf from around his face.

"What do you want?" Corvo asked. He was getting tired of these delays and was eager to get the men safely back to the barracks. Despite his bravado, Corvo recognised just how vulnerable he and Galba were. If they wanted to, the men could easily overpower the two of them and escape, though how far they'd get in their current state was debatable. He hoped that curiosity and the promise of a hot meal would be enough to persuade them to march without causing trouble.

"My name is Quintus Faustus, a guard from the quarry. I heard what you said to these men, and I would like to join you."

"Sorry, Faustus — I need killers, not boys," replied Corvo dismissively.

"Please, sir. I can ride and I can fight."

Some of the freed prisoners laughed and the young man's face turned crimson.

"Have you ever fought in a battle, Faustus?" asked Corvo, and Faustus shook his head. "Or killed a man?" Another shake.

"I'm sorry, Faustus, you'll be of no use to me, and you'll only go and get yourself killed."

"Please, sir, I'm pleading with you. There is no honour working for Seneca and his thugs back at the quarry. I want to better myself."

Corvo looked at Galba.

"We could use an extra pair of eyes right now," Galba said quietly, so none of the freed prisoners could hear him. "And I'll take the lad under my wing, show him what's what."

"Very well, on your head be it, Titus. Fall in at the rear, Faustus."

"Thank you, sirs. You won't regret it," beamed the young man.

"I already do," replied Corvo, trotting back to the head of the column.

CHAPTER 4

To Corvo's relief, he and Galba had managed to get all twenty-six men back to their makeshift barracks without anyone deserting and, more importantly, without any attempts on either his or Galba's life. Quintus Faustus had proved to be a willing worker who was keen to learn and please. Away from the oppressive and harsh quarry environment he was also proving himself to be quite intelligent, and his true personality was slowly emerging. Corvo had feared that one or more of the freed prisoners might try and slit the lad's throat, but it seemed they were content to largely ignore him, recognising that he wasn't one of the more brutal guards from the quarry.

Corvo's good mood was further enhanced when he found that in his absence Flavius and the others had worked hard to turn the dilapidated buildings into fairly decent living and eating quarters, with an area outside cleared for drill and weapons practice. He had also acquired the services of a cook, a man called Brutus who had served for over twenty years in the legions before being cashiered and who would brook no lip from the men around him. He also knew how to use a sword if it came to it, which it undoubtedly would.

"So your trip to the quarry was a success?" Flavius asked Corvo later that night as they shared a wineskin with Galba.

"Well, we have the numbers, but as to the quality of the men, only time will tell."

"And are you sure these men were worth rescuing?"

"I did not have a lot of choice, Lucius. You know this. The legate gave me little time and even fewer options."

"Who is this legate of which you speak?" asked Galba.

Corvo and Flavius exchanged a look.

"I think it's time you told him, Marcus."

Corvo rubbed his chin in thought and realised that he was sporting several days' worth of stubble, something he would have to soon remedy. "Very well, but it must go no further than this room, understood?" When Galba nodded, Corvo went on, "A few weeks ago, I was serving as an optio in the Eleventh on the Dacian border under Legate Publius Crispus. Our posting was coming to an end after a relatively quiet deployment, and everyone was looking forward to some leave. We had heard rumours of small bands of Dacians in the vicinity of our camp, but nothing to worry or threaten a legion. It turned out our intelligence was wrong.

"A week before we were to depart, just as dawn was breaking, a large force of Dacians attacked. We were caught unawares but quickly formed up, though their greater numbers meant that they were likely to prevail. Despite being an optio, I found myself in the centre of our front row. We were hard-pressed all along the line." Corvo paused to take a gulp of wine. "Then I did a foolish thing. I broke ranks and went forward to engage the enemy. The men followed and we were able to drive the Dacians back until they retreated."

"Bollocks! You might be a good soldier, Marcus, but you're a lousy storyteller," said Flavius, shaking his head. "I was there; I saw what he did. Our whole line was buckling and in some places there was only one reserve line waiting to rotate. The Dacians were starting to roll up our flanks. It didn't look good for us. Suddenly, Marcus shouts, 'Glory to the Eleventh', and rushes forward, swinging wildly and cutting barbarians down left, right and centre. Eventually he finds himself face to face with one of the biggest men I've ever seen. Marcus cut him down like he was nothing. Seeing this, our lads ignore the officers and rush forward to engage the enemy. I don't know if it was that or seeing this mad bastard covered in their chieftain's blood, but the Dacians' courage was spent, and they turned and fled. We cut them down by the score until the centurions ordered us back into line. This man single-handedly saved the day and probably all of our lives."

"I was foolish, reckless and undisciplined; I could have got us all killed by breaking the line like that," said Corvo ruefully. "A legion is nothing without discipline."

"Yes, but you didn't."

"What happened after the battle?" asked Galba, absorbed by the story.

"He received a hero's welcome in camp that night, but the next morning he was summoned to Legate Crispus' tent, where —"

"I'll finish telling my story, Lucius," Corvo cut in, "otherwise you'll embellish it and say I deserved a triumph through Rome, like Caesar."

Flavius spread his hands in supplication. "Maybe you did."

"I still don't understand what any of this has to do with this mission we're on," said Galba.

"I'm getting to that," said Corvo. "The next morning I was indeed summoned to the legate's tent. I fully expected to be stripped of my rank and flogged. The reason our armies are so successful is because of our discipline and training, and in one mad instant, I threw it all away and endangered myself and, more importantly, the lives of my brothers. I could have caused the whole line to collapse."

Galba waited patiently for Corvo to continue.

"As you would expect, the legate gave me the reprimand I deserved. There were two other men in the tent, another legate and a man I had fleetingly seen about camp on occasion but who wore no uniform. When the legate had finished his tirade, he turned to the others and asked, 'What do you think?' The other two men just nodded. I waited to hear how many lashes I was to receive and how long I'd be on latrine duty." Corvo paused and took a mouthful of wine.

"But?" prompted Galba, keen to hear how the story ended.

"But it turned out they had a different punishment in mind. The legate's son is a young tribune with the Fourth —"

"The Fourth? They're fighting in Armenia at the moment, are they not?" Galba interrupted.

"They are, along with a couple of other legions. I don't pretend to understand the politics of it, but it seems we and the Parthians wish somebody different to sit on the Armenian throne. The Fourth has apparently taken a mauling and a number of prisoners were taken, among them the legate's son, Gaius. General Corbulo commanding our forces won't countenance a rescue attempt. Legate Crispus won't give up on his son and tasked Cornelius Arus — the other man in the tent with the legate — with recruiting a small force to attempt his unsanctioned rescue."

"And that's where we come in?" said Galba.

"And that's where we come in," confirmed Corvo. "Instead of demoting and flogging me, they promoted me to centurion and tasked me with recruiting a small force to travel to Armenia and rescue Gaius. I was allowed to select a handful of regulars to assist me, but the bulk of my force had to be recruited from the prisons, mines and gutters. Expendable men. Whether we succeed or not, we will never get the recognition or thanks we deserve. If the emperor or Corbulo ever find out, we'll likely be disowned by Crispus to save his own career."

"And you volunteered for this?" Galba asked Flavius.

"I did. Mind you, I was drunk at the time."

"And now you've dragged me into this."

"To be fair, you didn't need a lot of encouragement."

Galba laughed. "No, I suppose not."

"Do you still want to be a part of this mission, now you know the full story?" asked Corvo.

"Of course," replied Galba. "But you do realise that by the time we arrive in Armenia, it will have been months since the men were taken prisoner and in all likelihood they will be dead? The Armenians have probably passed the prisoners on to the Parthians, and they aren't known for their hospitality. Just ask Marcus Crassus." The story of Crassus being taken prisoner by the Parthians a hundred years before, and having molten gold poured down his throat, was well known.

"I know, but we have to try."

Galba nodded. "So when do we leave?"

"Soon enough. But for now, I want you both to concentrate on moulding these men into a cohesive fighting force with whom we can entrust our lives, because where we're going, if we don't all work together, none of us will see these shores again."

"I think you need to work on your motivational speeches, Marcus," said Flavius, smiling.

"I didn't think you needed motivating, Lucius. Now listen, I have one more thing to attend to tomorrow, so while I'm gone get the new men kitted out with clothes and let them rest, or at least undertake light duties. We'll start to appraise their battle-readiness the day after. Understood?"

Both men nodded.

"Where are you going tomorrow?" asked Flavius.

"To see an old acquaintance," replied Corvo.

"Do you need another sword at your side?" asked Galba eagerly.

"Not this time, Titus. You stay here and help Lucius. When are the weapons being delivered?" The question was aimed at Flavius.

"Tomorrow, according to a messenger earlier today."

"Good. Distribute them as soon as they arrive."

Flavius stared at Corvo. "You want me to give the weapons to former prisoners, gladiators and dishonoured soldiers?"

"Yes."

"But —"

"There are no buts, Lucius. We need to demonstrate to the men that we trust them, because if we don't, how can we expect them to trust us?"

"As you wish." Corvo could tell that his friend wasn't convinced.

"I know the risk I'm asking you to take, but it's the only way. Keep your wits about you and make sure at least two of our regulars are on guard at all times, but don't let the others feel that they're prisoners again. As far as they are concerned, the guards are watching for outsiders approaching, not keeping them in. Understood?"

Both men nodded.

"One more question, Marcus. What if any of them ask to leave or attempt to leave by force?"

"It was made clear to the men that they either accompany us on this mission, or return to where we found them. There is no middle ground. If any of them employ weapons against you, they are to be killed without hesitation." Corvo gulped down the last of his wine and rose to his feet. "It's been a long day and I have an early start tomorrow. I'll see you both the day after tomorrow."

"That's if we haven't had our throats cut and our heads taken for trophies," grumbled Flavius as Corvo left the room.

Galba roared with laughter and slapped his young nephew on the shoulder. "You worry too much, Lucius. Let's have another drink. Tomorrow is going to be fun."

"Spoken like a true madman," said Flavius, smiling ruefully and holding out his cup.

CHAPTER 5

The next morning, Corvo was up before the sun. After quickly consuming a hunk of bread and cheese, washed down with a cup of watered wine, he set off for his destination. It was going to be another hot day.

It had been some years since, as an eighteen-year-old, Corvo had been sent to the Aquilla Training Camp just outside the city, but when he set eyes on it again it felt like only yesterday. Here, the new recruits were put through their paces and received basic instruction on drill, kit maintenance, and rudimentary weapons skills before being assigned to whichever legion required reinforcements. The training regime was hard and the conditions tough, deliberately so, as the legions wanted only the cream of Rome's manhood. Hour upon hour would be spent marching, learning how to seamlessly manoeuvre into certain formations, and fighting, with every weapon at the army's disposal. To toughen the recruits up, training was carried out with replica equipment which was deliberately heavier than the real thing. Having been prepared this way, the men would still be able to carry their equipment in the field when their muscles were burning and the rain had drenched them.

To deliver this training and maintain discipline, hard men were needed, and Corvo was here to see the hardest of them all: Optio Sextus Nerva. Corvo had hated Nerva during his long weeks of pain, humiliation and torment at the camp. The man took immense pleasure in breaking his charges before building them up again, ready to become valuable legionaries.

At the time, Corvo and his fellow recruits couldn't understand why Nerva drove them so hard, but now he knew.

He was just what Corvo's disparate group needed.

Having gained access to the training camp thanks to a warrant given to him by Arus at their first meeting, Corvo tethered his horse and made his way to see the camp commander. Without divulging any salient information, Corvo had requested that Optio Nerva be transferred to his command with immediate effect. The man had blustered at first, trying to project his authority on proceedings, but in the end he acquiesced, Arus' written orders making it a formality. Corvo had then wandered over to the main square, where marching and weapons' practice usually took place. Several groups of new recruits sweated in the morning sun as they were marched up and down by optios and other drill instructors. It brought back memories for Corvo, and he found himself wondering what had happened to some of the men he had trained with.

Corvo heard the man he was looking for before he saw him.

"What in Hades was that? I've seen drunks walk in a straighter line! What use will you lazy bastards be against barbarians? None at all! Now run round the square twice and then form two straight lines, and may Jupiter protect any man who fails to impress me this time. Well? What are you waiting for? Move, you lazy…" His voice trailed off as Corvo strode confidently across the parade ground towards him.

"Who in Tartarus are you and what are you doing on my parade ground?" Nerva bellowed, drawing inquisitive glances from some of the men sweating their way around the perimeter of the square.

Corvo came to a halt a couple of paces in front of him.

"Marcus Corvo! I thought I recognised that slovenly walk. Sent you back to basic training, have they?"

"You remember me?"

"I remember everyone, Corvo. Now, who sent you?"

"Nobody has sent me. I came to see you."

"Oh, and why is that?" asked Nerva. "Missing me?" Behind him, a squad of thirty recruits were shuffling into what they hoped would pass for two straight lines. Nerva's distraction had given them a welcome opportunity to catch their breath.

"I have a job for you."

"I have a job for you, *Optio*. I think you've taken a knock to the head, legionary, and forgotten your small role in this Empire. I'm the optio so I give you jobs, not the other way round."

"No, I think it is you who is confused, *Optio*. My name is Centurion Marcus Corvo, formerly of the Eleventh, now on a special assignment and you will therefore address me as 'Centurion' until ordered otherwise."

Nerva took a step towards Corvo and stared long and hard into his eyes. "And you can call me Andromeda." Some of the recruits behind him laughed. "Quiet in the ranks. Nobody gave you permission to breathe."

Corvo sighed. Reaching inside his tunic, he pulled out a small scroll and held it out for Nerva to take.

"What's this?" asked Nerva suspiciously.

"It's a warrant from my commanding officer addressed to *Centurion* Corvo, giving me permission to requisition whoever and whatever I need for my mission. Here, have a look for yourself."

Nerva hesitated and licked his lips.

"You can read can't you, Optio?" Corvo asked quietly, so the recruits couldn't hear. Nerva dropped his gaze. "Then shall I read it out for your benefit and that of the men behind you?"

Nerva brought himself to attention. "That won't be necessary. How may I help you, Centurion?"

"I think that you'd better dismiss your men."

Nerva spun on his heel and glared at the lines of recruits, who immediately snapped to attention.

"Better. But I want to see an improvement tomorrow. Now get out of my sight. Dismissed!"

With an audible sigh of relief, the recruits melted away to get something to eat and drink, out of the sun.

"So, what is it you want, Centurion?"

"Is there somewhere we can talk, Sextus? We're rather conspicuous out here."

"Yes, of course. Follow me, sir," said Nerva, adopting a more conciliatory tone.

A short while later, Corvo had given a broad outline of the eclectic group of men he had gathered and the role he saw the optio undertaking in training them. He gave no details of the mission they were all to undertake, only that it would likely be very dangerous, with little chance of success.

"And Titus Galba is with you?" asked Nerva.

"He is."

"A good man."

"I need more like him. Will you join us, Sextus?"

"Why me? I mean, I made your life miserable here. I would have thought I'd be the last person you'd want."

"You were just doing your job, I see that now. It helped mould me into the man I am today."

"And now you're a centurion?"

"I am. A field commission I earned fighting the Dacians."

"You've been to Dacia?"

"I was stationed on the border, and they launched a surprise attack. Thousands of warriors ready to tear our heads off came streaming over the ridge. It was a close-run thing."

"But you earned a field commission? You must have done something worthy of glory?"

"I did my part, Sextus, that's all. The real heroes deserving of the glory are buried over there. We lost a lot of good men that day."

"All I've seen for many years now are these four walls and an endless stream of recruits I'm supposed to convert into soldiers the Empire can be proud of. It's a thankless task, and I would like to see something of the world before my time is up. What about the commander here?"

"I've already spoken with him, and he was eager for you to … widen your experience and join us."

"Then I'd be happy to join you, Centurion. When do we leave?"

"There is just time for you to pack your kit and say your farewells. I will see you over by the horses when you are ready. I am going to find something to eat and drink in the meantime."

Nerva stood and hurried away to pack his possessions.

Corvo watched him go and hoped he'd made the right call. The last thing he needed was Nerva trying to bully any of the men. He needed him to be firm but fair. These weren't new recruits, but veterans who had seen more battles than Nerva could count. Corvo just needed him to mould them into a cohesive band of brothers who would die for one another. It wouldn't be easy, given their different backgrounds.

*

As promised, Corvo and Nerva arrived at the barracks early the next morning. It was clear from the grumbling that Corvo could hear as he rode in, that some of the men also remembered Nerva.

"Greetings, Marcus," said Flavius as he and Galba strolled out to meet him.

"Greetings, Lucius, Titus. How are things?"

Flavius gestured for two of the men nearby to come and see to the horses. "It's been eventful."

Corvo raised an eyebrow but didn't ask why. Instead he said, "This is Optio Nerva. He will be joining us as drill instructor. Optio Nerva, this is Optio Lucius Flavius and Centurion Titus Galba, whom you already know. Lucius, can you get someone to find Sextus a bunk and show him around?"

"Of course. Marius!" Flavius waved at a passing legionary. "This is Optio Nerva. Find him a billet and then show him where to get something to eat."

Marius nodded and gestured for Nerva to follow him.

"That's a strange choice," said Galba as he watched Nerva leave. "The man is almost universally hated for his treatment of new recruits. He'll be lucky if his throat isn't slit overnight."

"I'll have the skin off the back of any man that tries it," snapped Corvo. "I know he's not going to be a popular addition to our group, but he can enforce discipline and he knows how to convert a bunch of strangers into a functioning unit, and that's what I need right now. You and he know each other?"

"We served together at the start of our careers. The man I remember was a decent soldier, though I daresay years of training recruits has turned him soft and fat."

"Then perhaps you can reacquaint yourself with him? If the men see you two together and realise you are old comrades, they will be minded not to slit his throat."

"I'll do what I can."

"That's all I ask, Titus."

"Now that's sorted, let's get out of this damned heat and Titus and I can tell you what you've missed," said Flavius.

Corvo gladly followed the others into the cool building that had been assigned as the officers' quarters. Once inside, he collapsed onto the wooden chair and all but snatched the cup of wine proffered by Flavius. The contents were consumed in two huge gulps. Flavius raised an eyebrow and refilled the cup.

His thirst quenched, Corvo said, "So tell me, what news?" Flavius and Galba exchanged a look. "Come on, out with it."

"Two desertions overnight," said Galba. "Both Traianus' men. One was killed by a guard — he was armed, and the guard acted in self-defence. The other got away."

Corvo sighed. "It was bound to happen at some point. How's morale?"

"Surprisingly good. Neither man, it seems, was highly thought of. I don't think they'll be missed and I'm not sure that they were the sort of men we wanted watching our backs anyway, though I would like permission to go out and hunt the deserter down."

"There's too much to do, Titus. Justice will catch up with him eventually — the Fates will see to that," said Corvo.

Galba nodded.

"It does leave us two swords down, though," said Flavius.

"We'll try and replenish the losses on the way, but if we can't, we'll just have to make do with what we have. What else?"

"The weapons arrived, but no uniforms."

"I didn't order any. Where we're going, it's best if we try and blend in with the locals. Are the weapons acceptable?"

"Yes, there are more than enough for everyone, and not cast-offs either. Legate Crispus has made sure we got the best weapons available," said Galba.

"Excellent. And how's the cook?"

Flavius snorted. "Brutus? Well, his cooking hasn't killed anyone yet, so that's a bonus, but whether his lack of culinary skills are why the two men deserted, I couldn't tell you. The others, young Quintus, Drax and Atilus, are all settling in together. There has been the odd argument, of course, but Optio Nerva will soon put a stop to that, though I fear we have little need of him as a drill instructor."

"There's something you're not telling me, isn't there?" said Corvo. Again Flavius and Galba exchanged looks. "Speak."

"A stranger turned up here yesterday afternoon with a note from Legate Crispus. It seems he is to join us. Did you know about him?"

"No, who is he?"

"Cornelius Arus, or so he says. Won't tell us why he's been sent here, or anything, for that matter. He insists on speaking to you and you alone. He also insisted on being allocated his own room. He's waiting there for you now."

"You'd better take me to him, then." Corvo's grumbling stomach was going to have to wait a little longer, it seemed.

Cornelius Arus looked to be in his late forties to early fifties, with a receding hairline and clear blue eyes that shone with a keen intellect. He greeted Corvo warmly, as if Corvo were the visitor to the barracks, and not he. Corvo remembered him as the man who had been in the tent with Legate Crispus the day he had been given both his promotion and mission.

"Greetings, Centurion Corvo, it is good to see you again. Come in and take a seat." Arus gestured towards a small wooden seat opposite where he himself was sitting.

"Why are you here?" asked Corvo brusquely.

If the other man was offended, he didn't show it. "I'll be coming with you. As an observer and a facilitator mostly. I'm not here to interfere."

"Coming with us? As a spy, you mean?"

"Come, Centurion, there is no need for hostility. Yes, I will send updates back to the legate, but primarily I am here to help you in any way I can. I carry the legate's seal and will be able to requisition things for our journey. In addition, I can gain access to places you could not hope to go. No offence."

"None taken." Corvo's mind was racing. He could see the advantage of having Arus along, but he couldn't help but wonder if the man had a hidden agenda. "But you have already given me the warrant. Surely that is all the authority I need?"

"Ah yes, do you have that document?" asked Arus.

Corvo retrieved it from within his toga and passed it to Arus, who quickly opened it to verify it was the right document before tossing it into a small brazier. He caught Corvo's surprised expression. "Just destroying the paper trail. We don't want it falling into the wrong hands, do we?"

"And by wrong hands, you mean…?"

"Anybody who might seek to undermine our mission or seek advancement at the legate's expense. You understand, I'm sure?"

"But I may have needed that again."

"Well, in me you have the real thing."

"The journey we are undertaking will be hard, and I cannot afford to tarry waiting for anybody who is struggling," said Corvo eventually. "You understand?"

"Of course, Centurion. Don't worry about me — I'm more robust than I look. I won't be a burden."

"So long as we understand one another."

"I think that we do. When do we leave? The legate is keen for our mission to get underway. There has been no news of his son for some time, and he grows anxious."

"As well he might. Surely you both realise that the chances of his son still being alive are remote?"

"Perhaps. But the legate will not rest until he has definitive proof one way or the other. The man is staking not just his career but also his life on this mission. If the emperor were to find out…" He let the sentence hang in the air unfinished.

"Not just *his* life," Corvo replied with a sigh.

"So when do we leave?"

"As you will have seen, I have assembled my group. Many of the men are in a sorry state and need a few days to recover their strength. I only returned with the latest recruit about an hour ago. They need time to bond and build trust among themselves."

"Our mission doesn't have a few days, Centurion. They will have to build their trust on the march."

"Impossible." Corvo glared at Arus. "If I'd been given the regular troops like I asked, I could have complied."

"You forget your place, Centurion, and you forget mine," said Arus.

"I don't even know who you really are," said Corvo, "or how to address you."

A sly smile crossed Arus' face. "I am the legate's … fixer, shall we say. If there are things that need doing that the legate can't be seen to be involved in, I handle it for him. As for how to address me, Arus will do."

"No rank?"

"Not necessary in my role. However, make no mistake, I carry the legate's full authority."

"So who commands this mission, you or I?"

"You do … until you don't. I will grant you seventy-two hours to knock your men into shape, after which we march, regardless of the men's condition. Now, if you'll excuse me, I have a report to write." He gestured to the door.

Seething at being dismissed within his own barracks, Corvo got up and left without another word.

So much for not interfering, he thought as he shut the door behind him.

CHAPTER 6

Seventy-two hours had been nowhere near long enough for some of the men to recover. Nor was it enough time to meld the men into a unified fighting force, though it hadn't been for lack of effort on the part of Nerva, Galba and some of the old sweats. They had trod a fine line between pushing the men too hard and not giving them enough time to recuperate. The legionaries had soon fallen into step, years of routine embedded within them, but the gladiators were a law unto themselves. They knew how to fight better than any of the legionaries, and saw no need for drill instruction and defensive formations. Yet discipline and co-operation were the foundation of success for the legions. Consequently, the Roman war machine was peerless in the known world. Corvo had begun to question the wisdom of bringing gladiators along. In fact, he had begun to question the whole undertaking.

"Don't look so worried, Marcus. All will be well," Flavius said as they rode south-east towards the port of Brindisium and the ship awaiting them. It was their fourth day on the road.

"I'm worried about the former gladiators. They can fight, we know that, but will they stand in a disciplined line and watch their comrades' backs? I'm not so sure."

"You're worried they'll break ranks and do something stupid — like rush headlong into the enemy?" Flavius said with a smile.

"Point taken, Lucius. I was a fool. I cannot afford for them to follow my example."

"We knew it wouldn't be easy, given the composition of our company."

Corvo was going to question his friend further on this matter when he noticed they were approaching a village. For such a small place, there seemed to be a lot of noise coming from within.

"What in Jupiter's name is going on here?" said Corvo.

"Shall I ride ahead and check?" asked Flavius.

"No, I'll go. You bring the men. Split them into two squads. You come in from the main track and have Titus bring the rest in from the south, so that if there is any trouble, we can contain it."

Flavius frowned. "What trouble could there possibly be in a rural village in the heart of Italy?"

"I don't know, but it's best we're prepared. Besides, it will be good practice for the men." Corvo kicked his horse forward.

The village was home to a couple of hundred people, most of whom appeared to be gathered in the village square. Corvo climbed off his horse and began to push his way through the crowd, most of whom gave ground to the tough-looking stranger. On reaching the front, Corvo saw two men standing upon a wagon. One of the men had his head covered by a sack and was perched precariously on a small milking stool. A rope around his neck was looped over the branch of a large olive tree growing behind the wagon.

"What goes on here?" shouted Corvo. The other man on the cart, probably a village elder, Corvo reasoned, eyed the newcomer suspiciously and raised his hand for silence. The shouts and calls from the gathered crowd immediately died down.

Seizing his opportunity, Corvo asked again, "What goes on here? Why are you hanging this man?"

"You are a stranger here and this has nothing to do with you, friend," said the elder. Mutterings of agreement came from the crowd behind Corvo.

"What is this man guilty of?"

The elder glared at Corvo, who saw three men, strong and burly from working in the fields all their life, easing themselves through the crowd towards him.

"He is guilty of defiling a woman and then stabbing her father when he confronted him. Even as we speak, he fights for his life."

More mutterings from the crowd, angrier this time.

"If what you say is true, then it is a heinous crime indeed and his guilt or otherwise needs to be ratified in a court." The village men had closed in around him now.

"What court? There are no courts here, no magistrates. It is incumbent on us to deliver justice. Besides, his guilt has already been verified by his own words."

"Then let me hear it from his own lips," said Corvo, reaching beneath his cloak and pulling out his gladius.

Cries of alarm emanated from those closest to Corvo as they backed away, though the three men stood their ground. He knew that if they rushed him, they would in all likelihood overpower him.

"Very well," said the elder, and he removed the sack to reveal a beaten and bloody face. The village men had clearly already exacted some degree of revenge.

"Speak," ordered the elder, looking at the prisoner. "Tell him what you told us."

The prisoner lifted his head, taking in the hostile crowd in front of him. His gaze came to rest on Corvo and his eyes widened in recognition.

"Centurion?"

A surprised and worried rumbling spread through the crowd and the men surrounding Corvo backed away a couple of paces. The legions were known for looking after their own.

"Centurion Corvo, is that you?"

"It is. How is it you know my name?"

"It is me, sir, Livius Camillus. I came from the quarry with Traianus."

Of course, thought Corvo. *He's the missing deserter.*

"You know this man?" asked the village elder.

"I do. Is what they say true, Camillus?"

"It wasn't like that, sir. It was consensual. But her father had a pitchfork and was going to skewer me. I had to defend myself; I had no choice."

"I see."

"Please don't let them hang me, sir."

"I won't."

This drew angry mutterings from the crowd, which began to close in on Corvo again. Suddenly a cry of alarm went up; Flavius and the others had arrived.

Corvo gave a grim smile as he locked eyes with the village elder before issuing a one-word command: "Hem."

His men hefted their shields and locked them together by overlapping with the man to their left, forming two walls of shields. To Corvo's trained eye, it was a sloppy effort and something he would get Nerva to work on.

Corvo's men began to creep forward, compacting the crowd so that nobody had room to move, whilst Corvo nimbly leapt onto the cart to stand beside the elder. When he was satisfied the crowd were tightly confined, he gave the order to halt.

Corvo observed the crowd through narrowed eyes. "Prisoner Camillus has been accused of rape and attempted murder. These people were about to hang him without a fair trial. I cannot permit this." Some of Camillus' comrades nodded their approval. "However, aside from the things of which he is accused, he is a deserter and I made it quite clear at the outset of this mission that I would not tolerate any transgressions, and that if any were made, the perpetrator would either be returned to his previous circumstances or punished as I saw fit. If we cannot rely on one another, then this mission is already doomed. How can we succeed if we cannot rely on the man behind us to stand and not run at the first opportunity he gets? I will not let Camillus hang for the crimes for which he has been accused. But for deserting his post, I have no choice."

An audible gasp went up from the crowd as Corvo kicked the stool out from under Camillus' feet. The noose had not been skilfully tied, so rather than a quick, clean snap of the man's neck, instead he was slowly strangled to death. Eventually his body stilled, his eyes bulging and his swollen purple tongue protruding from his mouth.

A stunned silence hung over the village square, save for the gentle creaking of the rope as Camillus swung back and forth.

Corvo jumped down from the cart and made his way back towards the line of soldiers.

"Release!" shouted Corvo as he neared the perimeter, and his men instantly formed up into two rows. Perhaps they were making progress after all.

"Get these men moving again, Titus," said Corvo as he brushed past the big centurion.

Galba bellowed for the men to straighten up and march, and soon they were proceeding out of the village.

"Was that wise?" asked Flavius as he nudged his horse alongside Corvo's.

"I had to demonstrate to the men that I meant what I said. Camillus was already a dead man; I just used his fate to my advantage."

"He had friends among the men, Marcus — not many, granted, but a few. I could hear them muttering."

"Let them mutter. Now they know what fate awaits them should they choose to run. These aren't regular legionaries, Lucius. They are hard men; we just need to be harder."

Flavius nodded and they resumed the journey in silence. Arus sidled his horse up alongside Corvo.

"Well handled, Centurion."

"It was necessary."

"Indeed it was, but as Optio Flavius said, watch your back — there may be those who seek revenge." Arus turned his horse and resumed his original position in the column.

The rest of the journey to Brindisium was uneventful. The march had been slow and Corvo had found it hard to rein in his frustration at their lack of progress. Many of the men were unable to accomplish the twenty miles a day a fully kitted-out legionary was expected to manage, but as time passed the men appeared to be getting stronger and fitter.

To Corvo's disappointment the men had not bonded as well as he had hoped, with the former quarry workers banding together, former prisoners forming their own smaller clique, and the regular soldiers keeping their distance from all of them. The gladiators, both retained and freed, kept to themselves, a habit they had no doubt developed whilst inside their various ludi. After all, there was no point becoming friends with someone you might have to face in the arena and kill one day.

They arrived in Brindisium a couple of days ahead of their planned departure. It was a bustling town with many tempting distractions for the men, and Corvo wondered how he would keep them in check whilst they waited for their ship to be readied. Arus had gone down to the docks to try and hurry the preparations along, but returned later to advise Corvo that there was no way of expediting their departure.

"Half the crew are on leave and no doubt residing in the various taverns and brothels lining the docks. The captain is also awaiting some supplies. We're just going to have to wait," Arus said regretfully.

"So be it. A little rest will do the men good, so long as they don't take the opportunity to abscond."

"I will try and … incentivise the captain again tomorrow." Arus turned and melted into the crowd milling along the docks.

Later that afternoon, Corvo sat in his tent sharing a cup of wine with Flavius, Galba and Arus.

"You can't be serious?" said Galba, glaring at Corvo. "You want to let them wander the city unguarded tonight? They'll either desert or get themselves killed. Roll call tomorrow morning will be a very brief affair."

"If they were going to desert, they would have done so by now."

"I admire your trust in human nature, sir," said Galba, "but we haven't really been anywhere that offers the same temptations as this town."

"I agree with Titus. They can't be trusted," said Arus. Although the legate's man was a part of their inner command circle, Corvo still couldn't shake the feeling that there was more to him than met the eye.

"We have to trust them at some point. I say we let them have their fun tonight on the strict understanding that they are to be back here by first light tomorrow, when a full parade and equipment check will be carried out. After that, they can't leave camp again prior to embarkation. What say you, Lucius?" All eyes turned to the young optio.

"I think it's a risk, but I also think it's better to find out if we can trust them now on home soil rather than when we're in Armenia and potentially surrounded by enemies."

"A point well made, my friend," said Corvo. He looked at Galba and Arus. They both reluctantly nodded their agreement.

"Then it is agreed. Lucius, tell the men the good news. Arus, see to it that each man is given enough money to enjoy himself tonight without excess."

"I'm sure the legate will be delighted to hear that his money is being spent on cheap wine and even cheaper brothels," replied Arus bitterly.

"Tell him it was to boost morale."

"And will you be partaking of these … recreational activities, Centurion?"

"No. I have much to plan, but my comrades here may well be interested."

Galba and Flavius both nodded.

"Very well, I will see to it, but I hope you know what you're doing, Centurion."

So do I, thought Corvo to himself.

The news was well received by the men and Flavius actually received a cheer when he told them. By dusk that evening their makeshift camp was virtually empty save for Corvo, Arus, and five regular soldiers, two of whom guarded the camp while two others slept, ready to relieve them later. The fifth man was in his tent, suffering from a debilitating headache. All five, despite their disappointment at missing out on the evening's activities, were pleased to learn that they would still qualify for the monetary bonus the others had received.

Corvo spent the evening considering the mission ahead. His confidence was fast deserting him. He was a young, inexperienced soldier who was not used to being in command — why hadn't they chosen a more experienced man for the task? The answer was obvious: like the men he led, he too was expendable.

Corvo stared at the rudimentary maps, trying to predict every eventuality and problem he might encounter, but they were too many and his solutions too few. After a couple of hours he could feel a headache of his own coming on and decided to retire to his bunk for the night. Shortly after he closed his eyes, he was asleep.

He was shaken awake by Flavius after what seemed like no time at all and was surprised to learn that dawn had come and gone.

"The men are on parade, Marcus, awaiting your inspection," said Flavius.

Corvo gingerly sat up, expecting his head to hurt, but thankfully a good night's sleep had defeated the burgeoning pain.

"How bad is it, Lucius? How many did we lose overnight?"

"I think you'd better see for yourself, Marcus."

The news was obviously worse than he feared. Sighing, Corvo gestured for his friend to lead on and a few moments later he emerged into the bright morning sunshine to find their makeshift parade ground full of men.

"Roll call complete, Centurion. All fifty-eight men and officers present, including Tertius, who was bedbound yesterday," said Flavius, coming to attention.

Corvo couldn't believe his eyes. Not one man had deserted. Not even Traianus. His act of trust had been repaid.

He was just about to address the men when he noticed that many were sporting black eyes, cuts and abrasions of varying degrees of severity. It wasn't just the ex-prisoners or quarry workers, but the regulars and gladiators too. Even some of his officers, including Galba, displayed wounds of some sort. Corvo turned to say something to Flavius when a thud drew his attention back to the men. Someone in the front rank had dropped face-first into the sand, much to the amusement of his comrades. Most of the men were swaying on their feet.

"It looks like you had an interesting night, Lucius," said Corvo, raising an eyebrow.

"It was … entertaining."

"So it would appear. However, you seem to have returned my men in a damaged and fragile state and —" Corvo was interrupted by the sound of someone in the rear ranks vomiting. He sighed. "I suggest you get some food and water down them and then take them on a five-mile march to shake off last night's excesses." There were several groans from the men. "Make it ten miles if anyone else complains. Understood?"

"Yes, Centurion."

"There are to be no exceptions, apart from Tertius, who can remain here and guard our supplies along with another man of your choosing." Corvo turned and headed back to his tent, beaming widely.

CHAPTER 7

The forced march had the desired effect, and the men returned to the camp hot, hungry and sober. They were also extremely tired. After a brief rest there was yet another kit check and parade, followed by a hot meal. Brutus had described the food as his 'special', though he wouldn't be drawn on what it contained. Some of the men commented that they hadn't seen the camp mongrels all day and wondered where they'd got to. Too tired to complain, most of the men settled for an early night while the more hardy sat up sharing a wineskin and stories with Galba. The big centurion had laughed when the two dogs suddenly reappeared in camp, having evidently taken themselves off somewhere during the day.

After a good night's rest, the men boarded a cargo ship which had been converted to accommodate them, their horses having been sold to a trader in town. The ship's captain had been silenced with a generous bribe courtesy of Legate Crispus and backed up by a none-too-subtle threat from Arus.

Although there weren't many people on the docks at that early hour, those who were cast curious glances at the large number of armed men dressed in civilian clothes all boarding the same ship. Their ship slipped out of port with the early morning tide along with another, almost identical, craft. A mile out to sea, the two ships had parted ways and headed in different directions.

An hour out of port, Corvo was about to confront the captain regarding the direction they were sailing in, when Arus gently grasped his arm and led him to the side of the ship, away from listening ears.

"Is something the matter, Centurion?"

"I'm no sailor, Arus, but even I know Egypt lies to the south, yet I find we are sailing east. What are you not telling me?"

"I anticipated that our arrival and embarkation at Brindisium would draw attention, so I didn't tell anybody our true destination until we were aboard the ship, not even the captain."

"And just where is our true destination, Arus?"

"Macedonia."

"Macedonia?"

"We land there tomorrow. We will march to Thrace, where I have arranged for another ship to take us to Pontus. From there it's a short march to Armenia. Meanwhile, any spies will be waiting in Alexandria for an empty ship. By the time that ship docks and our ruse is discovered, we will be well on our way to Pontus."

Corvo turned to look at the ship that had accompanied them out of port and was now disappearing over the horizon.

"I paid that ship's captain to sail with an empty hold to Alexandria," said Arus. "He will tell anyone who asks that someone inquired about hiring his vessel but then changed their mind. He doesn't know where we are really headed, so even if they … question him, he cannot betray us."

"You really think there are people intent on disrupting our mission?"

"It's not so much about the mission as the people. The legate has enemies, and I have enemies too. There is always someone looking to improve their status, and to do that you need spies and informants."

"Can I share this new information with my officers?"

"Of course. They will recognise Macedonia when we arrive anyway. The men, however, can't be told until we arrive in Pontus. You can't trust them, Centurion."

"I don't trust you, Arus."

Arus smiled. "Then you are learning. Now, how are your men shaping up?"

"They grow stronger every day and will continue to do so as we march across the Greek mainland. There are still some minor antagonisms, but they seem to have bonded after their night out in Brindisium."

"Indeed. Quite some brawl, as I understand it. It cost the legate a considerable amount of money to make the authorities look the other way and release some of the men."

"I'm grateful for that. Whilst I don't condone what happened, the end result was that the men fought for each other, regardless of background. They are learning to live and work together as a unified force."

"Then perhaps it was money well spent," said Arus. "Besides, it is not me you need to thank, but Lucius and Atilus."

Corvo frowned. "How so?"

"Let's just say they may have planted the seeds of discontent that led to the fight."

Corvo raised an eyebrow. "So, what happens when we arrive in Pontus?"

"I have arranged for a guide to take us to Armenia. The situation on the ground will have changed since we set off, and my intelligence regarding how the invasion is going is stale; I need the guide to lead us away from any fighting — we don't want to be taken for deserters."

"And this guide will take us to the place where the tribune and his men are being held captive?"

"No. He will lead us to a tribal chief who has no love for the Parthians or the Armenians loyal to them. He and his men will assist in the rescue mission."

"And what's in it for them?" asked Corvo suspiciously.

"A free hand in the town or wherever it is the men are being held. Oh, and the chance to kill Parthians and traitors — it's a favourite pastime of theirs, apparently."

"Or they could be leading us into a trap," said Corvo.

"Yes, I suppose they could," replied Arus, smiling broadly. "All part of the job."

"If the men are still alive —"

"They are, according to my sources," interrupted Arus.

"If they are, then they're likely to be in a far worse state than some of my men were, and that's saying something. How are we meant to march them out across deserts whilst being pursued by angry Armenians?"

"There will be no pursuit if we execute this right. And let's be clear, Centurion, the mission is to rescue the legate's son, nothing more."

"I'm not leaving any Romans behind."

"You are if I think it will hinder our escape. Are we clear on that?"

Corvo pursed his lips and nodded.

"Good. Now, I think I'll retire for a few hours — we have a long march ahead of us when we land. We'll speak later." Arus turned and strode away.

Corvo watched him go. He had been surprised that Arus had managed to keep pace with the men on the march through Italy. Could he do the same again in Macedonia? In Pontus? Only time would tell.

Corvo turned and looked out to sea. So far the mission was going well, though he knew that the hardest parts were still to come. It had been months since the tribune and some of his men had been taken prisoner — surely they had either been killed or died of starvation by now. If they'd been sold as slaves, they could have been dispersed throughout the vast Parthian Empire. Death would surely be preferrable.

They made land late the following afternoon and after disembarking, set up camp a couple of miles inland, Brutus having bought enough provisions on their way through the town to feed the men for several days.

Arus and a couple of men had disappeared shortly after docking and returned a couple of hours later, each driving an ox and wagon. One was to transport the weapons and two were to be used as a food store and mobile kitchen for Brutus, for which he was grateful.

By the time the sun nudged over the eastern horizon the next morning, they were already marching due east towards a small port on the coast of Thrace.

The journey across the Greek mainland from Macedonia to Thrace took six weeks and covered a wide variety of terrain. By the time the men arrived, they were fitter and stronger than Corvo had ever seen them. They were also exhausted and irritable.

"Morale isn't great," said Nerva unnecessarily at that evening's officers' meeting. "We've been travelling for the best part of three months and the men still don't know why we're here. We risk losing some of them if we don't do something."

"Soldiers always moan. I'd be more worried if they weren't complaining," said Corvo.

"These aren't regular soldiers, Marcus," said Flavius. "We've done well to get this far, but I agree with Sextus — we're at a greater risk of desertion now than at any point since we left."

Corvo glanced at the others. Galba and Arus nodded their agreement.

"So what would you suggest?" asked Corvo.

"Permit them to let off steam tonight," suggested Galba.

"Another Brindisium?"

"It worked last time."

"I don't know if the legate's purse can stretch to buying off corrupt officials again," said Arus. "If you do this, you must make it clear that if they get into trouble, they're on their own."

"When are we due to sail?" Corvo asked Arus.

"Tomorrow, with the morning tide."

"Very well, tell the men they can visit the town tonight, but they must be back by *prima noctis hora.* If any are still absent by the time we embark, they will be considered deserters." The three officers stood up to leave. "One more thing: try and return my men in a better shape than last time or the sea journey isn't going to go well for them."

Flavius, Galba and Sextus nodded as they departed, leaving Corvo alone with Arus.

"The burden of command weighs heavy, eh, Centurion?"

"Something like that. Do you have any further news?"

"No. The next time I hear something will be when we arrive in Pontus, but even then, it will be days or even weeks old."

"And this guide you've arranged, you trust him?"

"Jupiter, no! Nor the tribesmen taking us to where our men are being held. But I do trust in the silver I'm paying them and in the fact that their hatred for us is a little less than their hatred for the Parthians and the men they consider traitors."

"That's comforting to know."

"Perhaps you should have declined the mission?"

"Perhaps I should, though it wasn't exactly made clear that I had a choice."

"Oh, you didn't, Centurion." Arus stood and slapped Corvo on the shoulder before heading for his tent.

Corvo was woken by the sound of a cart's wheels and the raised voices of several men. The noise grew louder as the procession drew up outside his tent.

"Centurion, I think you need to see this," called Galba from outside Corvo's tent.

Sighing, Corvo sat up, wondering what was so important that Galba felt the need to disturb him at this hour. Rubbing sleep from his eyes, he stepped out of his tent.

He could tell by the expression on both Galba and Flavius' faces that something was wrong. "Speak."

Flavius didn't reply but instead beckoned Corvo to follow him to the cart. Laid out on the back, covered by a sheet, were two bodies. Flavius pulled the sheet back, revealing the two men's faces. Corvo instantly recognised Legionary Tertius, who had missed the men's night off in Brindisium when he'd had a headache, and one of Traianus' men, whose name he couldn't recall. Corvo gestured for Flavius to cover them up again.

"What happened?" asked Corvo stonily.

"We all split up into groups when we reached the town," began Flavius. "My group, including Titus, came across an altercation as we were heading back. We could see some of our men were involved, so we ran to help them. Their attackers made off before we could reach them, but not before they'd stabbed these two. There was nothing we could do, Marcus."

"Were they alone?"

"Yes. They were originally part of a larger group, but these two decided to return to one of the venues they had visited earlier. What caused the fight I don't know."

"And what was all the shouting a short while ago?" asked Corvo.

"Some of the men want to get their weapons and go back to look for the men who did this," said Galba.

The gathered men began to voice their support.

"Silence!" bellowed Corvo. "There will be no revenge missions. You all knew the risks you were taking venturing out tonight. These men were foolish to separate from their group; they made themselves easy prey. If I knew who had done this and where I would find them, I would pick up my gladius and end them myself. But I don't, and I don't have the time to search for them; the tide waits for no man. We'll bury them here and then leave. I've lost two men already — I'll not risk losing any more. Optio Nerva."

Nerva stepped sharply to attention. "Centurion?"

"Arrange a burial party for these two men."

"Sir."

"Centurion Galba?"

"Sir," replied Galba, also coming to attention.

"Check that all the other men are accounted for and then get them to their tents. I'll not miss this tide. The sooner we're on our way, the better."

"Yes, sir," replied Galba.

Glancing once more at the covered bodies of his men, Corvo shook his head and returned to his tent.

In the end it was a close-run thing, and they only just made the tide. There had been a great deal of muttering and angry glances in Corvo's direction as the men boarded, though none dared to look him in the eye. It was clear they didn't agree with his decision to let their comrades' deaths go unpunished.

Well, they're going to have to live with it, thought Corvo.

"We're ready to cast off, Marcus," said Flavius.

"Then let's be on our —"

"Centurion, we have a problem," Galba cut in, joining the two men.

"What now?" snapped Corvo.

"The gladiators, Atilus and Decimus, they're not on the ship."

"But they came back last night. I saw them standing at the cart, looking at the bodies."

"I know. I checked everyone like you ordered. They must have left during the night."

"And the sentries didn't see them?"

"Apparently not."

"But why desert now? It makes no sense."

"We must leave now," said the ship's captain, a surly man with a scar down his left cheek. "Or we will have to wait for tomorrow."

"What do you want to do, Marcus?" asked Flavius.

"Damn it. We have no choice — we must leave. Cast off, Captain."

On the quay, two men began to untie the ropes securing the ship to the jetty, before hurling the ropes onto the ship's deck. A couple of sailors picked up long poles and began to ease the ship away from the jetty. At that moment they heard shouts.

Everyone turned to see Atilus and Decimus sprinting towards the ship, which was slowly distancing itself from the jetty. Both men were carrying a gladius and a small sack.

"Stop the ship," ordered Corvo.

The captain shook his head. "We are already running late. If we delay any further, we will miss the tide."

Corvo looked back at the running figures and realised that Atilus was getting ready to leap. Putting every last ounce of energy into his sprint, Atilus launched himself at the ship. A moment later he landed with a thump on the deck, his gladius spilling from his hand on impact and narrowly missing the ankle of a crewman, who cursed loudly in a language Corvo didn't recognise.

Atilus' fellow gladiator, Decimus, was not so lucky. By the time he leapt from the jetty, the ship was already too far out and he landed with an unceremonious splash in the sea, but not before he had hurled his sack onto the ship's deck.

"Get a rope to that man now!" yelled Corvo, but two ropes had already been thrown in Decimus' direction.

As Flavius strode over to where the man's sack had landed, Corvo watched as a couple of his men helped haul Decimus aboard, coughing and spluttering as he regurgitated half the Adriatic. It seemed that gladiators were not good swimmers.

Satisfied that the man was going to be all right, Corvo turned to see Flavius holding aloft a severed head. Atilus reached into his own sack and produced another. A cheer went up from the men.

"Where in Hades have you been and who were these men?" demanded Corvo, striding over to where Atilus was standing next to Flavius.

"These are two of the men who killed our brothers last night!" shouted Atilus, so that everyone aboard the ship could hear. The men roared their approval. "And none of their comrades will see another sunrise either." More cheering, then Atilus tossed the head and bloody sack overboard. Flavius looked at Corvo, shrugged, and then did the same.

"Atilus, a word," snapped Corvo. He turned and strode to the prow of the ship. Atilus followed. As he did so, the men all patted him on the back.

"What in Hades were you thinking?" demanded Corvo when they were out of earshot.

"I was thinking I'd get revenge for our fallen brothers."

"You disobeyed a direct order. I said there would be no revenge missions. You ignored that instruction."

"I am a free man, am I not?"

"You know full well that the moment you asked to join this mission, you were under my command, even as a free man."

"You are right, Centurion. I apologise. But I do not regret what we did. The men were not happy with you last night — they wanted revenge for their comrades, and you denied them that. You jeopardised all the hard work you had put into trying to mould these men into a unified force. Decimus and I have ensured that doesn't happen."

Corvo glared at the man as he considered his options. He was already four swords down. He couldn't afford to send Atilus and Decimus back and even if he could, how would he? The docks were now receding into the distance behind them. Begrudgingly, he had to admit that what Atilus had said about the men was true, yet he couldn't let his disobedience go unpunished.

"Sorry, Atilus."

"There is no need to —" Before Atilus could finish his sentence, Corvo's right fist connected with his jaw, sending him sprawling to the deck.

Atilus slowly got to his feet and wiped the blood from the corner of his mouth with the back of his hand. Activity on the ship had come to a halt as everybody watched the exchange, hands straying to sword hilts.

Atilus stared at Corvo and then nodded his understanding. Corvo had had to demonstrate his authority, and that was the only way.

"Atilus," Corvo said, "did you really get them all?"

"We did."

Corvo nodded and Atilus turned away, in search of a drink.

CHAPTER 8

Corvo closed his eyes and took a deep breath. It was good to be back on dry land, and once again he thanked the gods that he had been deployed to the legions and not the marines. The journey from Thrace to Pontus had been long, and although they had only encountered one storm, it had tossed their vessel about as if it was nothing, and many on board had been violently ill.

Mindful of the events in Thrace, Corvo had immediately led the men through the town, guided by Arus — the only person who knew where the guide would be waiting for them. They had eventually set up camp a couple of miles outside the town, at the bottom of some foothills. The arrival of such a large number of armed civilians in one ship had provoked much interest from the locals and authorities alike, and Corvo had been keen to get his men as far away from prying eyes as possible. The guide was due to arrive early the following morning, and Corvo decided that it was time he levelled with his men and told them about the mission.

Once the camp had been established and the men had eaten, Corvo called them all to gather round. Positioning himself on a flat rock where everybody would be able to see and hear him, Corvo studied the men before him. Once they had been a disparate bunch of deserters, gladiators, prisoners and other undesirables. Many had been weak and walked with the stoop of a beaten and disillusioned man. Now the men stood tall and strong. They were no longer a splintered group of cliques; now they were one force, their previous status forgotten. Gladiator mixed with deserter, who in turn mixed with former prisoners.

Even the handful of regular soldiers now accepted the others as their brothers. All they needed now was to prove themselves in battle. That time was coming.

"Men, we've come a long way, and I don't just mean from Rome, but as comrades. We've come to trust one another and soon we will have to put that trust to the test in battle." A loud cheer erupted. "It's time to tell you what I can about our mission." More cheering, but muted this time. The men were obviously keen to hear what the centurion had to say. "Tomorrow, we will be joined by an Armenian guide who will lead us deep into that country. As you probably already know, several legions of our brothers are already here fighting the Parthians over who is to rule Armenia, but that is not our concern. We will not be partaking in the war."

"If we're not here to fight, then why are we here?" called Traianus. Several other voices echoed his question.

"We're here to undertake a rescue mission." Corvo let the words hang in the air. "Some months ago, one of our legions came under attack and some of our brothers were taken prisoner, including the son of Legate Publius Crispus. Our job is to rescue him and get him safely home."

Muttering broke out amongst the men.

"Rescue *them*, don't you mean, Centurion?" somebody called out. "You said some of our brothers had been taken captive."

"Our mission is to rescue the tribune." Corvo glanced at Arus. "But, if at all possible, we will get all of our men out as well."

"Surely they will all be dead by now?" It was Drax, voicing the same concerns Corvo and his fellow officers harboured.

Arus stepped forward. "The latest information I have is that some of them, including the legate's son, are still alive."

"And how old is this information?" asked one of the regular soldiers.

"A few weeks old," Arus acknowledged.

Uproar followed until Galba bellowed for the men to quieten down.

"Then they could all be dead by now," said one of Traianus' men.

"Our guide should have more news for us tomorrow," said Arus.

"If we know where they're keeping them, then why doesn't General Corbulo send one of his legions to rescue them?" asked another of Traianus' men.

"It is not my place, nor yours, to question the general," replied Corvo. "I expect he is already hard-pressed and cannot afford the men he would undoubtedly lose in the attempt."

"Yet they're willing to let us die trying."

Corvo was beginning to regret briefing the men in such an open forum where they could freely air their views. "If you prefer, I can leave you in Pontus and arrange for your transportation to a mine nearby." The man shook his head. "I didn't think so. The general couldn't spare the men, nor in all likelihood would he have attempted it even if he did have sufficient men. This mission is not sanctioned in any way. Legate Crispus has put his position, his wealth, his very life on the line to try and save his son. The only men who could undertake this mission are men Rome won't miss — expendable men, like you and I."

"So you're saying that if we refuse, we'll be returned to where we came from or worse, and if we come with you, we're probably going to die?" asked Drax.

"I would have worded it slightly differently, perhaps, but essentially yes."

"Then we're damned if we do, and we're damned if we don't."

"Perhaps that is what we should call ourselves," said Flavius, stepping forward. "We are the Legion of The Damned."

Corvo nodded slowly, then shouted, "Glory to the Legion of The Damned!"

"The Legion of The Damned!" the men roared in response.

"Enjoy your evening, men — the real work starts tomorrow," said Corvo, turning and heading to his tent.

Early the following morning, their Armenian guide, Azarian, rode into camp. Corvo took an immediate and unaccountable dislike to the man.

"And there's no other way?" Corvo asked Azarian as he pored over the rudimentary map with Arus, Flavius and Galba.

"Not if you wish to avoid running into a patrol. Both the Parthians and Romans have armies in the area. The only way to avoid them is to go through the hills." The man spoke good Latin and for some reason he couldn't explain, this too irked Corvo.

"And how much longer will it take us to go through the hills rather than across the plains?" asked Arus.

Azarian stroked his jet-black beard as he considered his answer. "Only two extra days, three if men are slow; the going can be tough. They are called hills but are in truth more like mountains."

"Don't worry about the men. They'll be fine," said Corvo.

The Armenian nodded. "Then we should make good time."

"And you're sure our people are alive and well?" asked Flavius.

"Alive, certainly. Well? I could not say. Parthian hospitality is not the same as that of my people."

"But the town is garrisoned by your fellow countrymen, you said?"

"It is, but they are sure to be taking their lead from the Parthians."

"Very well. Any more questions?" Arus asked, looking around at the others. They all shook their heads. "Then I suggest we strike camp and depart immediately. You concur, Centurion?"

Corvo nodded, deep in thought. "I do. Titus, please give the order for the men to be ready to move shortly."

Galba nodded and left the tent to carry out his orders.

"If there is nothing else?" Azarian asked, looking at Arus. The Roman shook his head. "Then I will go and see to my horse, ready for leaving." Smiling obsequiously, he too turned and left.

"Are you sure we can trust him, Arus?" asked Corvo once Azarian was out of earshot.

"In my line of business you learn not to trust anybody. But I do trust in silver, and we are paying him handsomely to guide us. I think that will be enough."

"That's not very reassuring," said Flavius.

"Perhaps not, but it's the best I can offer, Optio."

"Well, I for one will be watching him closely," added Corvo. He nodded at his two companions and then he too left.

They had not long departed the camp when the complaints started. Some of the soldiers had served in places like Egypt, Syria and Judea and were therefore used to the stifling heat, but others, notably the former prisoners and some of the former gladiators, soon began to struggle. Corvo was pleased when their comrades, the more experienced hands, offered guidance and advice. They were finally working as a cohesive unit.

Neither Corvo nor Flavius had bought horses upon their arrival in Pontus. The wagons had been disposed of prior to leaving Thrace, despite Brutus' protests. Instead they marched alongside the men, enduring the same heat and dust. Only Arus and Azarian now rode.

Now and again the Armenian would ride off to scout ahead. He would disappear for quite some time before coming back smiling and looking refreshed, much to the disgust of Corvo and the dust-choked men. Corvo had suggested that Arus might like to accompany Azarian the next time, or at least let one of them borrow his horse so that they could keep an eye on the Armenian. Arus had refused, however, and told Corvo to relax and trust that all would be well. Corvo did neither.

As they neared the foothills on the second day, Azarian came galloping back and warned Arus that there was a patrol of Roman cavalry off to their east. The men were ordered to move quickly and quietly to a dry stream bed a hundred or so paces to their left, where they were to keep low and await further instructions.

"Why are we hiding from our own men?" Faustus asked Corvo as they hunkered down next to one another.

"We're not supposed to be here, remember? This mission has been ordered by the legate himself, not by the emperor. There would be awkward questions. It is more likely that they would just kill us."

"Kill us? But we're Romans. Well, most of us. Why would they kill us?"

"For a start, Quintus, none of us are wearing Roman uniforms, so they'd probably think we're deserters and execute us. More likely, given the clothes we are wearing, they could mistake us for Parthians or Armenian collaborators and attack us. They'll be looking for revenge after the mauling the legions took a while back. Either way, it doesn't end well for us."

"But we're carrying Roman swords and shields."

"They'd just think we'd looted them from the dead. Trust me, avoiding contact with them is for the best, at least for now."

The young man looked as if he were about to say something else, but Corvo put a finger to his lips to silence him. A few moments later, the faint sound of galloping horses drifted across the plain, getting louder. Corvo slowly raised his head to peer over the ridge of the stream bed and was shocked to see perhaps fifty Roman cavalrymen galloping towards them. Corvo hastily considered his options, none of which were good. Just when he thought they were bound to be discovered, the commander of the patrol veered south, leading his men away from where Corvo and his troops were concealed. They had come within a couple of hundred strides of them, and had it not been for the dry stream bed giving them somewhere to hide below ground level, they would have been discovered for sure.

Corvo watched the last of the cavalrymen disappear into the distance and released a long breath he hadn't realised he'd been holding.

There was a gentle whinnying, and Corvo turned in the direction of the sound. He was relieved to see that it was Azarian with his mare.

"We go now," said Azarian.

"What if they turn round and come back?" asked Corvo. "We'll be caught out in the open."

"Why would they? Besides, if they come back from the same direction, it's likely they'd discover us anyway," replied Azarian. "Stay in that gully much longer and you will roast to death."

He wasn't wrong, Corvo realised. It was as hot as Hades hidden in the relief.

"How long until we reach the foothills?"

"An hour if we hurry, and I think we should. Those Romans may have been running from something."

"Get the men up and moving, Titus," ordered Corvo, looking in the direction from which the cavalry had appeared. He couldn't see anything in the distance, but that didn't mean there was nobody there.

It wasn't long before the men were formed up and making best time towards the foothills. It was hotter than ever, and the sun bounced off the white sand, dazzling the soldiers, all of whom were hot, tired and hungry. This time, however, nobody complained and an hour later they came to a halt amongst some rocks and shrubs on the first hill. If either the Roman cavalry or Parthians showed up now, they would at least have a chance to conceal themselves from a casual search. The men at the rear of the column had done their best to disguise their tracks as they went, but they could not eradicate them entirely. The best they could hope for was to try and hide how many they were, and perhaps how recent the tracks were.

After a short break to drink and rest their weary shoulders, Corvo soon had the men on their feet and climbing again. Azarian assured him that a short climb further on was the ideal spot to make camp. They would be out of sight of anyone on the plain and concealed enough to light some small fires for warmth and cooking. Corvo would have liked to have scouted the site for himself, but time was not on his side, and he had no choice but to acquiesce.

By the time dusk fell, the camp was established, and several cooking fires were lit. Corvo had to admit that it was a good place to set up camp and his mistrust of Azarian began to ease;

perhaps his earlier sentiments about the man had been ill-judged. After posting guards both ahead of them and further down the trail, Corvo finally felt confident enough to get himself something to eat and drink.

"You need to relax, Centurion," said Arus, smiling. "We are concealed here, and you've posted sufficient guards."

"I would have preferred to establish a proper marching camp," said Corvo ruefully.

"Hardly practical up here. The ground is solid — there's no way you could get the men to build an earth rampart. Nor is it necessary."

"It's standard procedure. A proper camp with earth ramparts should be established every time a legion stops for the night."

"I know the rules, Centurion. I'm just saying they don't really apply here. There's little point in behaving like Roman soldiers if we're trying to hide the fact that that's who we are," Arus pointed out. Corvo sighed and his shoulders slumped as he recognised the truth in the other man's words. "You've done everything a commander could reasonably be expected to do. Now it is in the lap of the gods. Trust in them."

"I didn't think you trusted in anything except silver, Arus?" said Flavius, joining them.

"I don't, Lucius, but it doesn't stop me encouraging others to do so. Now, I think I shall rest. We have a long day ahead of us tomorrow."

"Before you go, where is Azarian?" asked Corvo.

"Further up the hill. He said he wanted to sleep up there so he'd have a better view of our surroundings when he woke and would be able to report back to us if he sees anyone."

Corvo looked at Flavius, who merely shrugged. It made sense to him too, apparently.

Arus stood and headed off to where he had chosen to sleep that night. Corvo noted that he had chosen a spot against the rockface, meaning nobody could approach him from behind. He wasn't that relaxed after all, Corvo mused.

"Get some sleep, Marcus," said Flavius. "Guards are posted and Titus has first officer watch. I'll relieve him and then wake you up later so you can take over from me."

Corvo yawned, then patted his friend on the shoulder and made his way over to where he was to sleep. After a few moments staring up at the star-filled sky, he was asleep. Around him, his men snored, played dice or spoke quietly in little huddles.

CHAPTER 9

The sun was bright when Corvo opened his eyes; it was going to be another hot day. After rinsing his mouth with lukewarm water, Corvo got to his feet and glanced around. The camp was buzzing with activity, the men busy either checking their kit, or finishing their morning meal. Corvo saw Flavius striding towards him, carrying a bowl in one hand and a cup in the other.

"Good morning, Marcus. I've brought you breakfast." He held out the bowl and cup.

"You never woke me, Lucius," said Corvo accusingly.

"You obviously needed your sleep, so I made the decision to take your watch too."

"You should have woken me. What example am I setting the other officers and men if I don't stand my watch? I can't ask them to do what I am not willing to do myself."

"Rank has its privileges, Marcus."

"I know, but I don't want to be that kind of officer."

"Well, you obviously needed to rest and you look far better today than you did yesterday."

"I feel it," conceded Corvo.

"Well, get that food down you. Arus is keen to be gone, as is Azarian." Flavius turned to go.

"Lucius." Flavius turned to face his friend. "Thank you." Flavius nodded and then strode away to oversee the striking of the camp.

A short while later, Corvo's men had once again started their passage through the hills. The gentle slopes soon gave way to steeper inclines, the path often narrowing so that only two men could walk abreast at any one time. Every now and again they would emerge onto a wider stretch of track, where Corvo and his officers would take the opportunity to check that none of the men had fallen by the wayside.

Occasionally, Azarian would vanish up the trail to check that the way was clear, returning shortly afterwards to urge the Romans to climb faster.

"What's the hurry?" Corvo asked him the third time he returned from scouting ahead.

"We are in dangerous country. It's better we keep moving," replied the Armenian.

"Dangerous how?"

"Bandits and brigands are known to roam these hills from time to time."

"Have you seen any yet?" asked Corvo, scanning the slopes either side of them.

"No, but that doesn't mean they're not there." The man looked genuinely afraid.

"Well, the men need to rest. How far to the next clearing?"

"A hundred paces, no more. But stopping there is a bad idea, Centurion."

"The men will be no good to anybody if we arrive at our destination exhausted and unable to raise a sword."

"Better than not arriving at all," replied Azarian.

"Lead us to the clearing and we'll take a short break for something to eat and drink. After that we'll push on hard."

"As you wish," replied the Armenian, but Corvo could see that the man thought his decision was foolhardy. Corvo glanced round once more as they resumed their climb. The hills were built for ambush. Bandits or even Parthian soldiers could be concealed all around them, just waiting for the right moment to attack, and they wouldn't know. The track was too narrow and its sides too steep to send out his own scouts, so his safety, not to mention the lives of his men, were being entrusted to this stranger.

Corvo and his men soon emerged onto a false flat. The area was approximately fifty strides wide. In front of them the path started to narrow once again and either side was flanked by low, steep slopes of loose stones and shale. Here and there oddly shaped boulders stood guard like sentinels in the clearing and the fittest of the men soon claimed these as their resting spots. Behind him, Corvo could hear Galba posting men to stand watch in both directions.

"These hills are harder to climb than they looked down on the plain," said Flavius.

"And full of places for an ambush," replied Corvo bitterly.

Flavius glanced around and nodded. "True, but we had little choice. Had we continued across the plains, we would have run into the enemy at some point. Here —" he waved his arm about to indicate their surroundings — "we at least have a fighting chance."

From the corner of his eye Corvo saw Azarian start up the trail they would have to use to continue their journey. "Now where is he going?"

"I've asked him to scout ahead again," said Arus, joining them.

"It's a pity he can't —" Flavius' words were cut off by two shouts of warning, one from in front and one behind.

"Form lines, form lines!" Corvo bellowed and immediately the men began to form up into two lines of equal length, facing each of the two entrances to the clearing. Between these lines the gladiators and those who had never served in the legions stood ready with their weapons. Corvo and Galba had taken up position in the southern facing line, and Flavius and Nerva stood at the centre of the northern line. All four were barking at their men to lock shields and brace.

The clearing had begun to fill with bandits, who had emerged from both tracks. One of the sentries watching the southern pass was down, having taken a thrust to the stomach from a spear. The other sentry had managed to fell two attackers and then quickly joined the shield line. Corvo did not know the fate of the sentries watching the northern track.

The bandits were poorly equipped, each man seemingly carrying a different weapon to his neighbour. These were not soldiers, Corvo was relieved to see, but opportunists, who must have spotted their progress and decided that they were an easy prey. They were about to learn their mistake.

The men were also poorly led. Although they had the advantage of numbers, by attacking them where they did the bandits were unable to funnel all their men through the narrow tracks at the same time, making their numbers initially worthless. Had Corvo been aware of their approach, he would have formed his men up in ranks of two at the entrance to both tracks, meaning that the enemy's numbers would have counted for nothing. Against trained legionaries they would have been scythed down in much the same way Leonidas and his Spartans had defeated the Persians at the Gates of Fire in Thermopylae. Nevertheless, this gave Corvo the chance to get his men into formation before the enemy had sufficient numbers in the clearing.

When the line was straight and tight, Corvo gave the order to advance. Some of the braver or perhaps more eager bandits had already thrown themselves against the line and had been efficiently and mercilessly cut down, the legionaries stabbing over their shields into the unprotected flesh of their enemy.

Slowly but surely the bandits began to give ground and fall back towards the path entrance, where Corvo knew his men would be able to hold them off indefinitely and eventually defeat them.

Perhaps sensing the Romans' plans, a shout in a language Corvo didn't recognise went up and the bandits hurled themselves at the Roman wall once again. The ferocity of their attack saw them enjoy some initial success. Corvo heard rather than saw one of the men to his left go down, only to be immediately replaced by a comrade from the line behind, whilst two of the former gladiators dragged the wounded man behind the lines.

Another man cried out to his right and Corvo spared a quick glance in his direction. The man had been stabbed in the shoulder but remained in the fight. Angered, Corvo gave the order to advance at pace. Putting their shoulders to their shields, they drove forward, trampling over the fallen as they did so. Every now and then a gladius would dart out from above the shields to stab at heads and necks. It was brutal Roman killing efficiency at its best and was too much for the bandits. In ones and twos the men at the back turned and ran for the track leading back down the hills until eventually their ordered withdrawal turned into a rout. That was their first mistake. Turning their backs on the Romans was their second. Trusting that the line Flavius was commanding was having as much success as his own, Corvo gave the order to break the line and the Romans poured forward to thrust steel into the retreating backs of the enemy, many of whom were now bottled up, awaiting the chance to access the track. It was a slaughter, the former gladiators finally getting the chance to bloody their weapons.

"Hold!" shouted Corvo when he saw that some of his men, their blood up, were intent on following the retreating enemy.

"Hold!" bellowed Galba.

Most of the men stopped and made their way back to the clearing, but it was clear that some had either disregarded the order or hadn't heard it.

Content that the enemy had withdrawn for now, Corvo turned to see Flavius thrust his blade into the stomach of a bandit. The last of the attackers were retreating up the track, away from the Romans, and Nerva was busy cajoling the men back into formation.

The ground in front of the Roman line was carpeted with the dead and dying. Corvo estimated that they had killed or wounded at least twenty bandits, although many had escaped and could return at any minute.

"Titus. Nerva." The two men hurried over to Corvo. "Get three ranks of men to block the entrance to the tracks. Then get me a casualty count." Both men nodded and departed. "Did any of your men follow them?" This question was aimed at Flavius, who had joined them after wiping his gladius clean on the tunic of a dead bandit.

"No, though they wanted to."

"Centurion!" a voice called from behind Corvo.

Corvo turned to see one of his men gesturing to him from near the entrance to the southern track. As he approached, the men ordered to guard the track parted to let two men stagger through. One was a former gladiator and the other a man they had liberated from a prison in Rome. The gladiator was bleeding from the top of his left arm, whilst he used his other arm to support his comrade, who had two arrows in him, one in his back and one in the left thigh. The wound in his thigh was bleeding profusely where an artery had been pierced.

Corvo had seen this before and knew the man was not long for this world.

"Set him down over there and get that wound seen to," Corvo ordered the gladiator.

"So they have a bowman, maybe more," said Flavius ruefully.

"So it would seem."

"We're lucky they didn't hide behind rocks and pick us all off one at a time. It's what I would have done."

"You're a Roman officer, Lucius, skilled in the ways of war. These are just bandits who thought that with superior numbers they could simply overpower us. I doubt they'll make that mistake again. We'll have to be extra vigilant from now on."

"Centurion?"

"What is it, Sextus?"

"I have the casualty count. Two of our men dead and three wounded, one of them seriously."

"And the enemy?"

"Seventeen dead and another five about to succumb to their wounds, sir," replied Nerva.

Over Nerva's shoulder Corvo watched as his men walked around the battlefield, finishing off the handful of enemy wounded.

"Then we've given them a bloody nose and they'll think twice about hitting us again, though I don't suppose that is the last we'll see of them. Tell the men to get a drink and rest while they can, but they're to keep their shields close by. We know they've got bowmen."

Nerva nodded and marched away to implement the orders.

"Nasty business," said Arus, taking in the sights as he approached Corvo and Flavius.

"It is. But why didn't your man Azarian know they were close? And where is he?"

"He did warn us it was dangerous, but I take your point. I will ask him when he returns from scouting ahead. He was probably unable to return because the bandits were between us and him."

"Or he led them to us and sat watching whilst our men died," suggested Corvo bitterly.

"Unlikely, but as I said, I will ask him."

They remained in the clearing for another hour, just long enough for all the men to have a drink and something to eat, the twelve men standing guard relieved halfway through so that they too could rest. Before they moved out, Corvo ordered that the bodies of the dead bandits be stacked up in the entrance to the southern track. It wouldn't provide much of an obstacle should the bandits decide to pursue them from that direction, but it might buy the Romans a brief respite. The man that had been wounded by arrows had died, making it three men lost. Their bodies were not added to the erstwhile barricade but were buried beneath cairns, the ground too hard to dig out any sort of grave deep enough to keep the mountain wolves at bay. By the time they were ready to depart, Azarian had still not returned, serving to further deepen Corvo's suspicion of the man.

There was only one track heading up the hill, so the guide's absence would not immediately be felt, but once they breasted the summit they would be at a loss as to which path to follow to their destination. Of more concern to Corvo was the fact that at least half of the remaining bandit force had retreated up the same path they were now climbing, and could be waiting in ambush at any point. His greatest fear was that they would use their bowmen to pick his men off one at a time, until they were so weakened they could not stave off another assault of the type sprung on them earlier. Nor did Corvo think it likely that they would stumble across another location so well disposed to defend against overwhelming numbers. It was with great caution that they resumed the ascent, each man doing his best to keep his heavy shield protecting his flank.

The men were understandably nervous and on two occasions somebody in the column shouted a warning, positive they had seen a bowman hidden in the rocks that littered the hill. The men had immediately squatted down, sheltering behind their shields, but when the tell-tale thump of arrows embedding themselves in the shields never came, the order to move was again given.

By the time the first arrows did come their way, the men's reactions were so sharp that not a single one of the score of arrows fired at them found flesh.

The second attack a little further up the track fared little better, though one legionary was nicked in the hand and another in the calf. Neither was a sustained or well-prepared attack and Corvo wondered if perhaps the bandits' supply of arrows was limited. With this in mind, he ordered that any arrows found were to be rendered unusable in case the bandits tried to retrieve them once the Romans had moved on.

Progress was slow. The men were tired from constantly having to heft their heavy shields and nerves were frayed at the thought of an impending attack. When Azarian suddenly appeared, he was fortunate not to be skewered by several gladii.

"Where in Hades have you been?" demanded Corvo.

"Apologies, Centurion. I was unable to return to you prior to the attack at the clearing as my way was blocked. I had been trailing the bandits and was expecting them to set an ambush further up the mountain, but they caught me by surprise and doubled back."

"And since then?" asked Arus.

"Since then I have been moving around and observing them."

"And what have you learned?"

"The men you drove off to the south are in pursuit. I was close enough to learn that they plan to attack you again a little further up the track."

"And how did this happen?" Arus pointed to a fresh cut on Azarian's right cheek.

The Armenian grinned. "I said I was close. One of them discovered me but was too slow to call out a warning. He speaks no more."

"And the bandits to the north, where are they?"

"They are camped further up. I do not think they will be harrying you again today."

"Then perhaps it is time we took the initiative," said Corvo thoughtfully.

"What do you have in mind?" asked Arus.

"We set an ambush of our own for the force to our south; that way, we can avoid being caught in a vice again. Then we climb and attack the men ahead of us, before they attack us."

"Here would be as good a place as any to deal with the men behind us," said Flavius, glancing around. "Besides, I think the men are too tired to push on and would rather stand and fight."

"Agreed. When do you think they're planning to make their move, Azarian?"

"From what I heard, towards dusk."

Corvo looked at the position of the sun. "Then we have just enough time to prepare." Corvo described to Arus, Flavius, Galba and Nerva how he planned to ambush the bandits. Both Galba and Nerva suggested small modifications, which Corvo approved, and soon the men were busy preparing the ground. Discreet lookouts were posted to warn them of the enemy's approach from both directions. Although Azarian had been positive that the bandit force to their north was camped for the night and didn't plan on carrying out any more forays until tomorrow, Corvo was not going to risk being taken unawares again. Nor did he entirely trust their Armenian guide.

As dusk began to fall, Corvo ran through the plan in his head. It was simple, but then the best plans usually were. He would split his force. Some would be formed up in lines at the far side of the clearing, commanded by himself and ready to receive the enemy attack. The few bowmen they had would be concealed behind boulders lining either side of the clearing, with a small reserve force of troops concealed behind them, commanded by Flavius. Atilus, Drax and the other gladiators, together with Galba, would find a place to hide further back down the track. They would then follow the enemy back up the track towards the Romans' camp. If all went to plan, the bandits would startle the sentries — who were under orders to immediately retreat — and burst into the camp, expecting to catch the Romans tired and unprepared. Instead they would immediately find themselves confronted by two lines of shields and swords. As they prepared to attack, Flavius and his men would assail them with arrows and rocks, sowing panic and disorder. Corvo's men would then advance, as would Flavius' reserves, meaning the bandits were hemmed in from three sides. Regardless of whether they decided to run or fight, the bandits would suddenly find their escape route cut off as Atilus and his gladiators attacked from their rear, essentially trapping them.

It was a good plan, Corvo finally decided, and he found himself praying that Azarian was right and the bandits would walk into the trap. He didn't have to wait long to find out.

The light was fading fast when the sentry sounded the alarm. As agreed, both he and his comrade immediately retreated without engaging the attackers. Buoyed by the belief they had caught the Romans by surprise, the bandits poured into the clearing, shouting their war cries. But the Romans were not sleeping or sitting around fires. Instead they were formed up behind a wall of shields at the far side of the clearing, the sentries having seamlessly joined them.

Before their leader could react, he and the other men who had been the first to enter the clearing suddenly found themselves being shoved forward as their comrades piled in behind them. Then arrows and rocks began to smash into them from their left and right. The braver men amongst their numbers hurled themselves at the Roman lines, but they were cut down by the grim-faced Romans, who were slowly advancing, the sharp steel of their swords flicking out from behind their shields like serpents' tongues and plunging into flesh.

The arrow and rock barrage ceased as two more lines of Romans strode down the loose shale on either side of the clearing. It was too much for some of the attackers and they turned to flee, only to find their way now blocked by yet more Romans. There would be no escape.

These bandits did not fight in the disciplined manner of legionaries and instead tore into their enemy with a brutal savagery. These were killers through and through, but still they stood no chance against the Romans.

The battle was soon over. Every bandit was either dead or dying, and those who had suffered a wound were soon despatched to the afterlife by the victorious Romans. Corvo's force had killed over thirty men and had not suffered a single casualty.

When Drax began to chant "The Damned" over and over, he was soon joined by the others until the chant became a roar.

CHAPTER 10

"Congratulations, Centurion, your plan worked remarkably well," said Arus, wiping his blade clean. Evidently, he had not sat this battle out.

"It did, and most importantly we didn't lose any men. However, this is only half of the enemy; the rest lie somewhere ahead of us."

"They do, and they can wait. They will not attack tonight, not if they've witnessed what has happened here. Enjoy your victory. Tomorrow is another day, another challenge." Arus nodded at Corvo and then headed off to speak to Azarian.

"What are your orders, Centurion?" asked Nerva, coming to attention in front of Corvo and saluting him.

"Post sentries front and rear, each group to stand guard for three hours. Detail work parties to throw the bodies down the slopes and then ensure everyone gets a decent meal and some rest."

Nerva nodded and turned to go.

"You did well today, Sextus. You all did. Let the men know, will you?"

"I will, but with respect, it might mean more coming from their commander."

"Yes, you're right. Thank you, Sextus."

Nerva smiled and then left to carry out his orders.

Once he was happy that sentries and lookouts had been posted in the right places, and he had managed to force down some food with the help of watered wine, Corvo took his officer's advice and slowly strolled round their makeshift camp, speaking to the men. He did not yet know all their names, but the fact that he was taking the time to speak to them was of more importance to the men. If Corvo had witnessed an act of bravery or disciplined behaviour and he could match it to a face, he commended the man. He had no doubt that a word of praise now would encourage the men to perform greater acts in the battles ahead.

"You men were ferocious today," said Corvo, coming to sit amongst the small group of former gladiators gathered around a fire.

"It is the only way we know how to fight, Centurion," replied Atilus. "You can try and drill us in the Roman way of fighting, but let us loose as we were today, and we will be far more effective for you than we are when stuck in a line surrounded by cautious soldiers." His fellow gladiators cheered their agreement.

"The men who stand in those lines are brave men too, Atilus. Never doubt it. It takes real courage to stand still and disciplined as the enemy comes charging towards you."

"It is not their courage I question, Centurion, just their ability. My men will kill more than yours if left to fight in the manner to which they are accustomed." His fellow gladiators nodded their approval once again.

"I doubt that we will be involved in a pitched battle where formations are necessary — at least, I hope not. But you all fought well today. Drink, laugh, but get some rest. There will be more blood to spill tomorrow, I expect."

The gladiators all cheered as Corvo got to his feet and wandered off to the next small group of men. It was late by the time he had managed to speak to everyone and Corvo was struggling to keep his eyes open. He was about to lie down and try to get a few hours' sleep when he noticed the silhouette of a man sitting on a boulder by himself. It was Faustus, the young guard who had deserted his position at the mine to join Corvo's band.

"Quintus? Are you all right?" asked Corvo as he approached the young man.

"Centurion. Yes, I'm fine." It was obvious from the look on his face that he was very far from fine.

"You fought well today, Quintus. Many have said so."

"They did?" The lad sat up a little straighter. The part about people commenting on his bravery wasn't true, but Faustus had acquitted himself well and a small lie was sometimes all that was needed to get a soldier back on an even keel.

"They did. How did you feel? It was, after all, your first battle."

"I felt..."

"Terrified?"

"To my great shame, yes," replied Faustus, unable to meet Corvo's gaze.

"Well, don't be. You don't think we were all scared before our first battle and every battle since? If any man here tells you otherwise, he is a liar. Apart from Galba — I'm not sure anything scares him except his wife. She is a fearsome woman, apparently."

Faustus laughed and Corvo saw the tension drain from his shoulders. "Even the gladiators? I don't think they're scared of anything."

"Believe me when I say that every man has his fears; some just conceal them better than others."

"And what about you, sir? Were you scared?"

"Of the battle? No. Of making the wrong decision and letting my men down? Yes. When you're in command, you feel a responsibility for each and every man you lead. The deaths of the three men in the earlier ambush already weigh heavy on my conscience. One day perhaps you'll understand."

"I can't unsee his face."

"Whose?"

"The man I killed today. The first man I killed."

Corvo nodded. "Nor will you. I can still see the face of the first man I killed, and many of those since. Their shades haunt my dreams."

"Does it ever get easier?"

"It does. But never forget, it is better that his body lies as food for the carrion than yours." Faustus nodded, but Corvo wasn't convinced the lad understood everything he had tried to tell him. "Now, why don't you get some rest? We've got a long day ahead of us tomorrow."

The sky to the east was just starting to lighten when Corvo had the men stand to. There had been no further incidents during the night and none of the lookouts had reported seeing the enemy. Corvo wondered if perhaps they had withdrawn, gone to hide whilst his men passed through the mountains, but it was unlikely, he realised; this was, after all, their home. They would no doubt know the fate of their comrades and would likely be seeking revenge.

Azarian had estimated that the men camped further up the mountain numbered no more than forty, meaning that this time the Romans had the numerical advantage.

There would be no ordered battle lines for this attack. Surprise was to be their main weapon. Corvo had split his force into three. He would lead a force comprised of Atilus and his gladiators, as well as some of the more ill-disciplined men under his command. Their job would be to storm the camp as quickly as possible, sowing panic and confusion. It was just the sort of one-to-one fighting Atilus and his fellow gladiators would welcome. Flavius would then follow with a squad of men to stop any bandits from attempting to flee down the mountain. Finally, Arus and a few others would follow, bringing up everyone's equipment. All those involved in the assault would carry nothing but their weapons. Arus had not appreciated his role in the plan, but had acquiesced when Corvo had pointed out the alternatives.

Guided by Azarian, Corvo and his section started to silently climb the path, the men ordered not to speak or make any noise whatsoever. It was not long before Azarian gave the signal to stop and Corvo gestured for his men to hunker down.

"What is it?" Corvo asked Azarian.

"Their sentries are just round this corner and their camp no more than forty strides beyond that."

Corvo and Atilus exchanged a surprised look. "You did not tell us they were this close," hissed Corvo. "They could have fallen on us at any time."

"I told you I could see they were making camp for the night. You were safe."

Corvo was angry. They had been anything but safe and had he known the bandits were so close, he probably would have withdrawn his men.

"It is no matter, Centurion. We're here now," said Atilus. He was obviously keen for a fight.

Corvo gestured for two Syrian brothers he had recruited from one of the many prisons to come forward. Like many of their fellow countrymen, they were renowned bowmen.

"Just round this corner are —" Corvo looked to Azarian for confirmation, and the Armenian held up two fingers — "two sentries. I need you to take them out without a sound, if possible." Both men nodded their understanding. "Tell the men to make ready," Corvo then whispered to Atilus. When he was satisfied that everyone was ready, he gestured for the two Syrian bowmen to creep forward. When they were mere inches from revealing themselves to the sentries, they glanced round at Corvo, awaiting the order to release. Corvo closed his eyes briefly and readjusted his grip on his gladius. Then he nodded to the Syrians.

The brothers were every bit as accurate as Corvo had hoped. In one fluid movement they had leapt into the middle of the track, giving them sight of the sentries, and released their already nocked arrows. Shocked, the sentries had stared at them wide-eyed before slumping to the ground, one with an arrow squarely in the middle of his chest, the other with an arrow through his throat. Neither had uttered a sound before dying.

Corvo glanced around the corner to check that Azarian's estimate of how far away the sleeping bandits were was accurate, and then, satisfied that the Armenian's information had been correct, he gestured for the men to follow him. The Syrians were to take up positions on either flank and pick off anyone who tried to run.

The Romans crept silently forward, and Corvo began to believe that they were going to reach the camp without being spotted, but he had long considered that Fate was fickle. When they were no more than twenty paces from the heart of the camp, one of the bandits chose that moment to wake and go and relieve himself. He had stood open-mouthed, staring at Corvo and the others, not quite sure what he was seeing. As realisation dawned, he opened his mouth to shout a warning just as an arrow hit him in the chest. This time, however, it was not a killing shot, and the man was able to cry out a warning before a second arrow silenced him forever.

Then all of Hades broke loose.

The man's shout had woken many in the camp and they quickly reached for their weapons, but it was too late. Atilus and the others were already amongst them, cutting throats and stabbing down on those too slow to rise from their slumber. One-on-one skirmishes broke out, but the bandits were no match for either the gladiators or Corvo's legionaries. Some were quick to realise this and tried to flee north, only to be felled by Syrian arrows. Others tried to run past the Romans back down the mountain, but they soon found themselves confronted by a wall of impenetrable shields as Flavius and his men entered the camp, penning the bandits in.

It was another slaughter and soon there were just four bandits left standing. Only one of Corvo's men had fallen. The bandits threw down their weapons and dropped to their knees.

"We cannot take any prisoners," Arus said to Corvo, when he and the detail emerged into the camp.

"I know," replied Corvo. The thought of having to kill these men in cold blood left a bad taste in his mouth, but he knew Arus was right. It would only take one of them to report that a small force of Romans disguised as locals was heading into Armenia and there would be all sorts of people searching for them. "Dispose of them and let's be on our way."

Atilus and three other gladiators had taken up positions behind the kneeling men, ready to slit their throats. Arus slowly walked along in front of the prisoners, Azarian at his side. "Do any of you have anything to say that might convince me you should live?" Azarian translated Arus' words. "No?" Arus nodded at the gladiator behind the first kneeling prisoner and in one swift movement, the man pulled the prisoner's head back by the hair and sliced his gladius across his throat before letting his lifeless body drop to the ground. "How about you?"

Arus asked the second man, his words again translated by Azarian. This prisoner simply met Arus' gaze and spat on the ground at his feet. The gladiator behind him didn't wait for the signal, instead quickly despatching his prisoner in the same manner as the first.

The third prisoner in line began hurriedly speaking in his own language.

"What is he saying?" Arus asked Azarian.

"He says that they haven't left the hills for a long time, but they have seen passing columns of soldiers less than a week ago heading southwest."

"That is of no use to me. Ask him if he knows anything about Roman prisoners and where they are being kept."

Azarian translated. "He says there are rumours that they are kept at a place called Vermuk."

"How far away is this Vermuk, and in which direction does it lie?" Arus waited for his question to be translated and then for the answer.

"He says it is no more than four days' march to the east."

"The east?" queried Corvo. "But we're heading north."

"Ask him —" Arus' words were cut off by the fourth prisoner, who was clearly telling his fellow prisoner to be quiet.

"Ask him if Vermuk is to the east or the north," said Arus, but he was now staring at the fourth prisoner, who glared back at him in defiance.

"He says he has nothing more to say," said Azarian. Whatever his fellow prisoner had said to him had obviously been enough to secure his silence.

"Then he is of no more use to me," said Arus, and a quick nod to the gladiator standing behind the prisoner was enough to see the man swiftly sent to the afterlife.

"And what of you? Have you anything to say?" asked Arus of the remaining prisoner. The man glared icily back at Arus. "No? You had plenty to say to your comrade a few moments ago. If you don't speak, you'll soon be joining him."

"I will soon be joining him whether I tell you anything or not."

"So, you speak Latin. That makes things easier. If I give you my word that you will be set free if you tell me something of importance, will that loosen your tongue?"

"You Roman dogs lie. It has been so long since any of you spoke the truth that you no longer know the difference," spat the prisoner. His gaze was fixed on Azarian.

"This is your last chance," said Arus.

"My people will one day rid ourselves of both you accursed Romans and you Parthians and once again be free."

"There are no Parthians in our company," said Arus.

The bandit snorted in derision. "Even when it is before your very eyes, you —" His words were cut off as Azarian swiftly produced his dagger and sliced the man across the throat. The gladiator holding him let go of his body, and he too crumpled to the ground.

"You might have let him finish," Arus protested.

"Apologies, but he is … was … a traitor to my people and offended me."

"Why did his comrade say that Vermuk is to the east, not the north as you would have us believe?" asked Corvo.

"He is right — Vermuk is to the east, but to get there you would have to cross a lot of open plains where you are sure to be spotted. My way is longer but reduces the chances of you being discovered."

"Surely you mean *us*, not *you*. If we're caught, you'll be caught too," said Arus, raising an eyebrow.

"Quite so."

Arus returned to Corvo's side.

"Did you learn anything useful?" Corvo asked him.

"No, just another puzzle."

Corvo waited for the other man to elaborate, but it seemed he was not planning on doing so.

"Then we will bury our man and continue on our way."

Arus nodded but did not reply. He was deep in thought.

After building another cairn for their fallen comrade, Corvo led his men up the track a little after midday. Azarian had gone ahead to check the path, but had assured Corvo that the bandits had been destroyed and they had the hills to themselves.

Corvo had been pleased with how the men had performed in the minor battles they had fought since entering the hills, but he knew that what they would face at Vermuk would be a different proposition altogether. Morale was good and the men were finally thinking of themselves as one force. Even Traianus was being less objectionable with each passing day, not that Corvo trusted him.

By late afternoon they had crested the summit of the hill and Corvo had given the order to make camp for the night. To attempt to descend in failing light on paths they didn't know, where a stumble over a loose rock could send a man tumbling to his death, wasn't a risk he was prepared to take.

The views from the summit were spectacular. To the east, vast open plains stretched to the horizon, punctuated by small rocky outcrops and what looked like a small oasis. To the north, gentle rolling hills stood as sentinels on the other side of a narrow plain, which might take a couple of hours to cross. To the west and far in the distance, Corvo thought he caught the glint of the sun on the distant sea. Somewhere out there stood the fortress town of Vermuk, where the tribune and an unknown number of Roman soldiers were last known to be held captive.

"Quite a view, isn't it?" said Arus as he approached Corvo.

"It is," replied Corvo without turning.

"The Armenian prisoner reckoned it would take perhaps four days to reach Vermuk across the plains. Azarian thinks going through those hills will take perhaps a week but will be the safer option. What do you think?"

"If we run into trouble out on those plains, there's nowhere to run, nowhere to hide. We'd be caught out in the open and slaughtered. Much as I am eager to reach Vermuk, there's no point in putting ourselves in unnecessary danger for the sake of perhaps two or three days. Do you agree?"

"I do. Azarian will scout those hills at dawn and report back, but he says bandits don't use them. We'll see what he has to say when he gets back."

"Very well. I will check our sentries and then retire, and I would urge you to do the same, Arus. The days ahead could be hard," said Corvo, smiling amiably.

"Thank you, Centurion, I will."

Corvo nodded and after one last glance at the hills they would likely be climbing the next day, he set off to ensure the sentries were alert and in place before settling down for some much-needed sleep.

Corvo was woken from a fitful and unrefreshing sleep just after dawn by a stern-faced Galba. "Sorry to wake you, Centurion, but we may have a problem."

Corvo was instantly awake. "What is it? What has happened?"

"Arus is missing."

"What do you mean, missing?"

"He's not in the camp."

"Then he's probably squatting behind some rock somewhere trying to pass whatever concoction Brutus punished us with last night. My own insides feel like they are going to rebel at any moment."

"We've looked, Centurion. Unless he takes his privacy very seriously and has travelled halfway down the mountain to relieve himself, he's nowhere around."

"What about the sentries? Did they see anything?"

"They claim to have seen Azarian leave, but not Arus."

"How is that possible? He's not exactly young. He couldn't have sprinted past them."

"I couldn't say, Centurion."

Faustus appeared and offered Corvo a cup of wine and some cheese and dried biscuits.

"Best I can do, I'm afraid, Centurion," he said apologetically.

"My gratitude." Corvo took a couple of large mouthfuls of wine and then broke off a piece of cheese. He was deliberating on what to do about Arus when a sentry came running over and reported someone was approaching. Galba and Flavius hurried over and the three of them turned towards where the man was pointing. "Is that Arus?"

"No point asking me. I can barely see the man, let alone identify who he is," grumbled Galba.

"Remind me to never surprise you, Titus, especially if you happen to be holding a pilum," murmured Flavius to the centurion. "I don't want to be skewered in a case of mistaken identity."

"Probably best," agreed Galba, stern-faced.

"Well, is it Arus?" snapped Corvo.

"Yes, it is," replied Flavius. By now the man had nearly reached their camp and even Galba could make out Arus' features.

Despite his age and the slight climb, Arus appeared to be barely out of breath when he arrived in front of the cluster of officers. He too gladly accepted a cup of watered wine from Faustus and nodded his thanks.

"Where in Tartarus have you been?" demanded Corvo.

"I went out scouting."

"Isn't that what we're paying Azarian for — to check the way ahead is clear?"

"I wasn't scouting the route," replied Arus. "I was following Azarian."

"What? Why?" asked Corvo.

"I had my reasons."

"And you didn't feel it necessary to share them with me?" snapped Corvo.

"I didn't want to share my concerns without proof."

"And how about now? Do you have proof to verify your concerns?"

"I do."

"Someone is approaching!" shouted the sentry.

"Who is it?" asked Corvo.

"Looks like the Armenian guide, Centurion," replied the sentry.

"Let him through when he gets here." Corvo turned back to Arus. "You were saying?"

"I followed him. What that bandit said yesterday about the truth being in front of us and his reference to Parthians, it got me thinking."

"So you followed him…?" urged Corvo.

"I did. I waited for Azarian to go and shortly after I crept out after him — I got past your sentries alarmingly easily, by the way. I followed him to the foothills, never once giving my position away."

"And what did you see?" asked Flavius.

"What I saw was our friend Azarian meeting up with a large force of Parthian cavalry. And they met as friends."

"What? Where did this meeting take place?" asked Corvo.

"Just beyond the ridge of that first hill. The ground falls away, providing a nice spot to hide what must be nearly two hundred cavalrymen."

Corvo took a deep breath. "That means our way is cut off in that direction, and if we try and cross the plains, they will race out from their hiding place and slaughter us in the open."

"I think that might have been the plan all along," stated Arus.

"He's Parthian?" asked Galba, horrified.

"I believe so, that or an Armenian sympathiser. Either way, he is no friend of ours," said Arus. Then, in a low voice, he went on, "He approaches. Say nothing, any of you. I will deal with it in due course." He turned to the Armenian. "Ah, Azarian, there you are. I was beginning to think you'd deserted us."

"Apologies, Arus, I ventured further into the hills than I intended."

"And did you find anything of concern?"

"Nothing. The way is clear. No bandits, no Parthians, not even any Romans."

"Excellent, you have done well, Azarian. Do you still think we will reach Vermuk in six days' time by following that route?"

"I do."

"That is good to hear. Go and get something to eat and drink. It will not be long before we move out again, I suspect."

Azarian bowed and walked away.

"Do we even trust him that Vermuk is in that direction?" asked Flavius.

"It is, and it's not as far as he says either."

"Then we have no need of him. Let us dispose of him now and be done with this treachery," said Corvo.

"All in good time, Centurion. You never dispose of an asset until they can serve no further purpose. In fact —"

Arus' words were cut off by the arrival of Atilus.

"What is it, Atilus?" asked Corvo.

"You're going to want to see this for yourself, Centurion."

The men followed Atilus as he led them to the side of the camp that looked out onto the huge plain that Azarian had said would be the quickest but most dangerous route to Vermuk.

The sight that greeted him took his breath away. Thousands of Armenians were lined up in battle order, facing south.

Behind him, he heard Galba curse.

A strange thumping noise was gradually getting louder, and they all turned to look at the slight rise about two miles to the south. Coming over the ridge in neatly drawn-up cohorts, their armour glinting in the sun, were thousands of Roman soldiers. As they watched, more and more men emerged to take up their positions in the battle formation.

The legions were here.

CHAPTER 11

"That complicates matters," said Flavius matter-of-factly as he watched the two armies.

"Actually, I think it simplifies things," replied Corvo.

"How so?"

"Well, there's no possibility of crossing the plain now, so we either go through the hills where Arus saw the cavalry, or we sit here and wait it out."

"Waiting is not an option," said Arus.

"Neither is going through those hills. We'd be walking into a trap, outnumbered four to one by cavalry. They'd slaughter us," protested Flavius.

"Yes, but at least we'd know they were there and have a fighting chance," said Corvo. "We'd have no chance out there." He pointed to the plain. "If the Armenians don't kill us, our own side are likely to, dressed like this."

Across the plain, the Roman legions were still marching into a pre-ordained battle formation with quiet efficiency; it was an astonishing sight, and Corvo and his men watched intently as their brothers-in-arms prepared for battle. By comparison, the Armenians had drawn up in what appeared to be rough order.

"Can you see which legions are down there? Is it Corbulo?" Corvo asked.

"Looks like one legion and several cohorts of auxiliaries," replied Flavius.

Somewhere in the distance, from the Armenian side of the plain, a horn sounded and with a great roar, the colourfully adorned host started to move forward, slowly at first, and then picking up speed as they closed in on the Romans. From the flanks, cavalry raced forward and began raining arrows down on the Roman lines. The Romans, however, were well prepared and at a well-timed command, the legionaries overlapped their shields so that they were protected both in front and overhead. Most of the arrows thumped harmlessly into the roof of shields, but the odd arrow squeezed through a hole to pierce the flesh of an unlucky soldier.

When the hail of arrows ceased, the men behind the fallen dragged their stricken comrades out of the line and took their place, whilst the Roman archers took their opportunity to pepper the withdrawing enemy archers. The horsemen did not have the luxury of shield protection and consequently many men and horses were cut down. These were not the famed archers of Parthia who had decimated Crassus' army in the previous century. The Armenian archers withdrew to the rear of their forces as their infantry now broke into a run, slamming into the Roman front line like a wave smashing on the rocks.

The disciplined and stoic Romans braced against the initial onslaught and then began to push back, their gladii flicking over and under their shields, finding flesh. The efficient killing that the Roman legions were known for now began in earnest against the lightly protected Armenians. It looked to Corvo as if the Armenians outnumbered the Romans by at least three to one, but the Roman army had overcome worse odds in its long and bloody history.

"Time we were going," said Corvo, turning his back on the battle. "Get the men moving, Titus." When Galba didn't immediately respond, Corvo repeated, "Titus?"

"They're going to lose."

Corvo glanced over his shoulder at the battle unfolding behind him. He could see that the Romans were indeed being driven back now that the Armenian archers had rejoined the fray.

"We cannot help them. What difference would fifty or so men make? None. We'd just add to the body count." Corvo put a hand on the big man's shoulder. "We all feel as you do, but on this occasion our mission must come first."

"I have never run from a fight, and walking away now doesn't seem right, that's all."

"There is no sense in us dying too."

It hadn't been Corvo who replied, but Traianus, who had overheard their conversation.

"But then you'd know all about running away from a fight, wouldn't you, Traianus?" said Galba.

"You weren't there. You don't know what happened," snarled Traianus, squaring up to the big centurion.

"Oh, but I was. I was in charge of the party guarding the Eagles. I witnessed how you and the other spineless maggots in your century refused to advance and help our beleaguered comrades."

On several occasions over the previous months, Traianus had thought he recognised the big centurion, but could never quite place him. Now the truth suddenly hit home, and he stared at Galba, wide-eyed. "It's you. You killed my friend Pollus!"

"Yes, and I would have killed more of you had I the chance."

"I'm going to kill you, you miserable…"

"Enough, both of you!" bellowed Corvo. "Centurion Galba, get the men moving; I've made my decision. Traianus … walk away."

With one last glare at each other, the two men parted.

"That's something we may have to resolve," said Flavius to Corvo.

"It would be better if they resolved the matter themselves, but not now, not here. Now I need them both focused."

Flavius nodded his agreement, and then something over Corvo's shoulder caught his attention.

Corvo glanced round, looking for what had distracted his friend. "What is it, Lucius?"

"Look." Flavius pointed.

Corvo's eyes widened when he noticed scores of horsemen galloping from behind the hill on the other side of the narrow plain towards the Armenian army. They had evidently either been ordered to join the battle or had decided greater glory was to be had by joining the fight than springing an ambush. The way ahead was now open.

Corvo smiled. "Get the men moving, Lucius, but not a word to Azarian. Tell the men they are to move quickly and quietly and not stop until we reach that hill."

Flavius nodded his acknowledgement. He was smiling too. It seemed that today the gods truly favoured them.

"You've seen them too, I take it?" said Arus, striding over to Corvo.

"Indeed. It is an opportunity we cannot waste."

"Fortune is smiling on us today. Look, they seem to be massing their cavalry and those riders who were lying in wait for us have been ordered to join them. It looks like they're going to try and roll up our flanks. Whoever is in command down there needs to withdraw, and quickly."

Corvo nodded. "All the more reason for us to hurry."

Galba came striding over. "The men are ready to go, Centurion."

"Then let's not delay," said Corvo. "We have wasted enough time already."

Quietly and efficiently, the men under Corvo's command descended from the small plateau on which they'd been watching the battle and started to cross the plain towards the hill opposite. There was no way of knowing whether all of the Parthian cavalry had left to join the battle, but any lookouts remaining could be dealt with swiftly. There was also no way of knowing whether Azarian had noticed the riders deserting their hiding spot. Corvo hoped not.

Although the battle was taking place out of sight around the eastern face of the mountain, the sounds of clashing steel and the screams of dying men were clearly audible and many kept glancing in the battle's direction, perhaps half-expecting a troop of cavalry to catch them in the open. If they did, they would be easy prey to the Armenian cavalry.

"That's it, Brutus was the last man," said Flavius, panting heavily as he finished the count a short while later.

Corvo nodded with satisfaction. They had made good time and had crossed without anybody falling or injuring themselves. More importantly, their passage had gone unnoticed. Even Arus had crossed the plain speedily; in fact, he'd beaten a number of younger men across, though it was true he wasn't as weighed down by equipment as some of them.

No shouts of alarm had gone up as they made the base of the hill. Azarian had suggested they climb over the ridge and out of sight to where he thought the Parthian cavalry still waited. Corvo had agreed and told Azarian to lead the way, which he seemed keen to do. When he was just a few paces from the top, Azarian broke into a sprint but came to an immediate stop when he reached the summit. He looked anxious when the others joined him.

"Is all well, Azarian?" asked Arus.

"Yes … yes, of course," the man stuttered in response.

"Only you look surprised."

"No, I am just relieved that there were no soldiers hiding here."

"Surprised … or disappointed?" pressed Arus.

It took only a quick glance at the cold expression on Arus' face for the Parthian to realise that he had been found out. His right hand slipped towards his sword, but before he could grasp it Arus had produced his own dagger and sliced it across the man's throat. Wide-eyed, Azarian moved his hand over the gaping wound from which blood now pumped through his fingers. Wordlessly, he dropped to his knees and then fell sideways onto the dirt.

Some of Corvo's men stared, not understanding why their genial guide had suddenly been killed. Corvo was not minded to tell them, not yet. Right now he had to secure their surroundings and allow the men a brief rest. The sprint across the plain in the heat had been taxing. There was also no guarantee that once they'd taken part in the battle, the Parthian horsemen wouldn't return, hoping they were still in time to cut the Romans off.

"Nerva, pick some men and hide Azarian's body somewhere where it won't be easy to find," ordered Corvo.

Nerva nodded and pointed at two men. They retrieved Azarian's body and carried it a little further up the slope. Shortly afterwards, Nerva hurried back down to where Corvo was sitting, having a drink by himself.

"Centurion."

"What is it, Sextus?"

"The battle hasn't gone well."

"How do you know?"

"I climbed onto a flat rock and looked back in the direction of the hill we had left. From there I should have been able to see the Armenian lines."

"And?"

"They're no longer there, sir."

"Then we've given ground, and the Armenians are in pursuit."

"So it would seem, sir."

"Any sign of the Parthian cavalry heading this way?"

"No, sir."

"If the battle has gone as badly as we fear, then the Armenians are likely to press home their attack, but there is always the chance that the Parthian cavalry may be ordered back to try and intercept us. Give the men a brief pause to gather their breath, and then we must climb."

"If they do come, sir, they'll know we've been here. The tracks of fifty men are hard to disguise."

"There's not much we can do about that. We'll just have to take our chances."

"News?" asked Arus as he ambled over to where Corvo now stood, deep in thought.

"The battle does not appear to have ended in our favour. The Armenians are in pursuit, but that doesn't mean they won't double back and come after us."

"Then we should be on our way."

"Indeed, but before we go, tell me, what made you suspicious of Azarian?"

"I'm suspicious of everyone, Centurion. I became suspicious of Azarian when the bandit prisoner said we couldn't see the truth even when it was before our eyes. He knew Azarian was a Parthian, and that's why Azarian silenced him before he could say any more."

Corvo nodded. "Well, let's hope that we can find Vermuk without him."

"Let's hope that we get the chance," added Arus.

"On your feet, The Damned. It's time we moved," ordered Corvo. Flavius, Galba and Nerva immediately took up the call, ordering the men to get up. There was audible grumbling and muttering, and Corvo smiled to himself. Now they were soldiers. With one last look in the direction of the battle, Corvo turned and started to lead his men up the hill.

CHAPTER 12

It was their second day in the hills and Corvo began to relax. There had been no signs of pursuit by a cavalry detachment, though the soldiers at the back were under strict orders to keep watch behind them and report any sightings immediately.

The terrain over the rolling hills was much the same as the hills they had previously crossed, but the tracks were wider, without the treacherous falls on either side, and despite their constant grumbling the men were making good time. Azarian had told them that it would take two days to cross and descend the hills, before reaching a small open plain, after which they would arrive at a river whose crossing would likely be guarded. From there it was little more than half a day's travel to the fortress town of Vermuk.

Corvo had wondered at the accuracy of the Parthian's directions, given that he'd had no intention of taking them any further than the hills they were now traversing, but he reasoned that the man had nothing to lose by being honest. The truth was no use to a dead man. Besides, providing a detailed description of their proposed journey gave Azarian more credence.

"Marcus," said Flavius as he fell into stride alongside his friend, "the men will be no good to us if they're all dead on their feet by the time we get to Vermuk. They need to rest. We all do."

"I know. Once we've breasted that ridge, we'll stop." Corvo pointed to a ridge about four hundred strides away.

Flavius nodded but didn't say anything. Corvo could see by his expression that he had something further to say.

"What is it, Lucius? What troubles you?"

"When their cavalry return empty-handed, they're going to know we're still out here. How in Hades' name are we supposed to breach a fortress town when their soldiers are on the lookout for us? We'll never get near the town, let alone inside it."

"I have a plan." It wasn't Corvo who had replied but Arus, who had sidled up behind them unnoticed. He was making a habit of that.

"If you have, then it's news to me," snapped Corvo.

"The fewer people who know, the better."

"And you didn't think that the commander of this mission should be one of those few? Who else knows about your plan?" asked Corvo.

"Just me. I was going to let you know soon," said Arus.

Corvo held up his hand, signalling for the column to stop and fall out. The sighs that greeted his command indicated it wasn't a minute too soon. Around him he could hear Galba and Nerva giving orders to the men and posting sentries.

"So what is this plan, Arus?"

"We have men on the inside."

"Spies?"

"No, Armenians, loyal to Rome."

"And how do we know we can trust them? I thought Azarian was your man, but that didn't turn out to be the case."

"Azarian was a late addition to my plans and one I regret. The men waiting for us on the inside are the same tribe as the men who are going to help us take the town."

"So you don't know them?"

"No, but I believe we can trust them. They despise the Parthians."

"And when are we to meet these men who are going to aid us?"

"All in good time, Centurion."

The two men glared at one another until Corvo took a deep breath. "As you wish."

"How much further is Vermuk?" asked Flavius.

"On the far side of that plain below is a river," said Arus, pointing. "We have to cross that, traverse a small forest and then we are but a couple of hours' march from the town gates."

"Assuming we manage to cross yet another plain without being seen, how will we cross the river?" asked Corvo.

"The only way to do so is via a small bridge, which will be guarded by at least four men, though since the war broke out this may have changed."

"And the approach?"

"Trees to one side, open on the other."

"Then we are going to need a diversion whilst some of the men infiltrate the trees and take the sentries down with arrows," said Corvo. "Aside from the Syrians, are any of the men competent with a bow?"

"Depends how long the shot. If it's close, then probably. Some acquitted themselves well against the bandits. If it's a longer shot, then I'm probably the best bowman you've got," replied Flavius.

"We'll have to wait until we're closer and assess the distance. Whatever happens, none of the sentries can be allowed to escape and raise the alarm or we truly are damned," said Corvo.

"How long do you think it will take us to cross the plain, Centurion?" asked Arus.

"Azarian estimated two days, but the men are fitter now and with the right motivation we could do it in a day. Why?"

"Then might I make a suggestion?"

"By all means."

"Rest here now, and then tonight, when it gets dark, we'll cross the plain and take to the trees. We'll rest during the following day and then take the bridge around dusk, when the guards' thoughts have turned to wine. Hopefully, we'll catch them unawares."

Corvo looked at Flavius, who shrugged. "Makes sense to me."

Corvo nodded. "Very well, let's tell the others."

As soon as it began to get dark, Corvo carefully led his men down the hill and started to cross the plain. Corvo had the men secure everything likely to clink or rattle before they left. Talking was to be kept to an absolute minimum and only if essential.

The sky was cloudy, the moon only occasionally managing to peek through before retreating once again. The lack of moonlight would help Corvo's men to remain hidden from view, but would also slow their progress, as visibility would be limited. They would have to use the torches and campfires of the bridge guards to direct them. They couldn't risk torches of their own, as their approach would be seen from far off and the Armenians would be able to get a rider away long before Corvo's men were close enough to take them down with arrows. Consequently, they only just made the safety of the trees before the sun rose. From where he crouched, Corvo could see two guards standing watch at the bridge whilst their comrades slept. They looked bored. After posting guards of his own, Corvo gave orders for the men to rest and eat. They would attack at dusk.

Corvo himself managed to grab a few hours' sleep, but by mid-afternoon the heat was too great to sleep through, even in the shade of the trees, and after checking his kit he studied the bridge and its guards. No one tried to cross the bridge from either direction, and Corvo began to understand the guards' boredom.

"Atilus! Flavius!" Corvo hissed. The two men crept forward until they were alongside Corvo. "Atilus, do you think you and your men can take the bridge?"

Atilus stared at the bridge, now guarded by five men. "We can."

"Be quick and be quiet. We don't know if there are more guards nearby, so be watchful. Flavius and the Syrians will take care of the three guards at the far end of the bridge, but you're going to have to deal with the two men at this end. The Syrians will watch your backs. And Atilus … no heroics. I can't afford any more casualties."

Atilus nodded and hurried away to brief the men. Flavius, meanwhile, crept off to find the two Syrian brothers. After he'd explained what Corvo wanted, the three of them quietly began to pick their way through the trees until they were as close as they could get to the far end of the bridge. After checking their bows, each nocked an arrow and watched the bridge.

Corvo explained the plan to Galba and Nerva, and when he next looked towards the bridge, he saw that Atilus and the gladiators were only a few paces from the two guards. Neither were aware that death stalked them as they chatted to one another. Now was Atilus' chance. Suddenly a sixth guard appeared from underneath the bridge, adjusting his breeches.

He froze and raised his hand to point before calling out a warning, but it was already too late.

Drax and Decimus rushed up behind the two guards, grabbing them around the neck and then running them through with their gladii. Both guards dropped to the ground. The guard who had been relieving himself had reached for his bow and after quickly dipping an arrow into a nearby brazier, fired it into the sky. The next moment he crashed to the ground, struck on the back of the head by Atilus, who had crept up behind him. The arrow, fired in haste, plunged harmlessly back down to earth.

At the other end of the bridge, both Syrians had made kill shots, their arrows striking the guards in the centre of their chests. Flavius' arrow had caught his target in the neck, leaving a nasty gash but not killing him. Somehow the Armenian had the presence of mind to rush to where their horses were tethered and quickly mounted one.

Watching from his position in the trees, Corvo cursed. The man was going to escape and raise the alarm. The rider had just turned the horse towards the town when a spear struck him in the middle of his back and he fell heavily to the ground. Corvo watched as Decimus ran to catch the horse, tethering it with its companions once again.

Corvo's mind raced. Unless Arus' intelligence was wrong, and they were much closer to the town than they thought, the warning arrow could not have been meant for those within the town. Which meant that there were more enemy soldiers stationed close by. Roaring at his men to follow him, Corvo drew his gladius and sprinted from the cover of the trees. They had to cross the bridge before Armenian reinforcements arrived.

"Everybody over the bridge now! Prepare for an attack!" shouted Corvo as he rushed past the two gladiators, the men following in his wake. Soon everyone was standing on the far side of the bridge, facing the woods. On the other side and across a small plain lay the town holding the tribune.

Corvo had the men form two double lines, with the archers on the flanks and the gladiators in the middle. If a large force of cavalry burst out of the woods now, they would have no choice but to retreat and try and hold them off on the narrow bridge.

When no Armenian reinforcements came howling from the trees, Corvo began to believe that the signal may have gone unseen.

The Armenian Atilus had knocked senseless was just starting to come around. When he saw that he was surrounded by enemy soldiers, the man began to speak rapidly in his own language. Corvo didn't need to speak the man's tongue to know he was begging for his life. Drax raced over and pulled back his head, ready to slice open the man's throat.

"Stay your hand, Drax!" bellowed Corvo. For a moment it looked as if Drax was going to disobey Corvo, his blood clearly up. One of the Syrian brothers — whose name Corvo had learnt was Kochar — instantly nocked an arrow and pointed it at Drax. "Let him go, Drax," Corvo ordered. "I have questions."

"You would kill me over him?" demanded Drax.

"I would, as I would anyone who disobeyed my direct orders."

Drax spat on the ground and flung the prisoner forward, before storming off.

"We are going to have a problem with Drax at some point," said Flavius, ruefully.

"Just say the word and I will end your problems," said Atilus. "He is not popular with me nor my brother gladiators."

"He may yet have a use," said Corvo. "Now, let's see what this wretch has to say. Do you speak Latin?" he asked the Armenian. The man stared back at him blankly. "Kochar, do you understand him?"

"No, Centurion, but my brother Sherko speaks a little Armenian."

"Then fetch him."

The Syrian nodded and returned a minute later with his brother.

"Sherko, Kochar says you speak some Armenian?"

Sherko nodded.

"Please ask this man if he knows anything about Roman prisoners and where they are being kept."

Sherko spoke to the prisoner in what sounded like a close approximation of the other man's language.

"He says that he doesn't know anything."

"Tell him that he is of no use to me then, and I shall give him to Drax."

Again Sherko translated, and the look of horror that crossed the Armenian's face didn't need explaining. Then he started talking — a lot.

"He says that he has heard rumours that Roman prisoners were taken after the Romans marched out of their forts along the border and crossed over into Armenia."

"I'm not after a history lesson. I want to know where they are and whether they are still alive."

Sherko translated again, struggling with some of the words which he had to repeat before the prisoner fully grasped what he was asking.

"He says that the prisoners are being held at Vermuk. He's not sure how many, but one is of importance to the Parthians."

Corvo nodded. It could only be the tribune. "Now ask him where Vermuk is and how long it will take us to get there. I also want to know how many soldiers there are."

Sherko nodded and asked the questions. "He says that it is less than a day's ride to the south."

"And how many men are stationed there?"

"He says nearly a thousand," said Sherko after questioning the man and waiting for his answer.

"Let's try this again," said Arus, stepping forward. He took out his dagger and sliced the man's cheek. "Tell him that I know Vermuk lies to the east, not the south. I also very much doubt there are a thousand soldiers guarding a handful of Romans. Tell him he has one chance to tell the truth, or my next cut takes out his eye. Tell him I am not a patient man."

Sherko began to translate. The man started talking, his eyes never leaving Arus' dagger, and Sherko had to tell him to slow down so that he could understand what he was saying.

"He says that he was mistaken and yes, Vermuk is to the east, and we should reach it tomorrow. The garrison numbers change depending on whether any of the king's men are passing through and stop for resupply, but the standing garrison is around three hundred."

Corvo and his officers exchanged a look; it was more than they had anticipated.

The prisoner started to laugh.

"What in Hades does he find so funny?" asked Flavius, but before Sherko could ask there was a shout of alarm from one of Corvo's men.

"Here they come!" The Armenian signal had been spotted after all, it seemed.

"Tighten those shields!" bellowed Corvo and immediately the men in the two lines overlapped their shields and braced to receive the enemy. The two Syrian brothers clasped arms and then took up positions at either end of the lines, whilst Atilus and his gladiators gathered behind and between the Roman lines. Their job would be to exploit any vulnerabilities in the enemy's attack.

The mounted Armenians came thundering towards the bridge. Without waiting for a command, the two Syrians and Flavius began firing arrows at the attackers, all three of them finding a target as the enemy came at them in close formation.

"Javelins." The order came from Galba. "Release."

The second rank released twenty or so javelins, almost all finding a target, be it horse, rider or the mass of foot soldiers following behind the cavalry. There was no time to release a second volley, however, before the cavalry slammed into the front line of Romans, a sea of flesh colliding with a wall of shields.

Standing in the centre of the front line, Corvo felt the line shake and give, before slowly reasserting itself. Realising there wasn't room to fight on horseback, the Armenian cavalry had either dismounted to fight on foot, or had forced their way back through their own lines to fire arrows from the rear. Their messy withdrawal had sown confusion and disarray in their own ranks. Now the killing could begin in earnest.

The Armenians hurled themselves at the Roman line, probing for weaknesses in the Roman wall, but finding few. Every now and again an Armenian arrow would find a gap and pierce flesh and the Armenians would surge forward, but the gap was quickly plugged by a legionary from the rear rank, and his gladius would flick out above his shield to stab an unwary Armenian in the throat or face.

The Armenian losses were mounting, but still they came and as Corvo ducked behind his shield to avoid a sword thrust, he could see that there were too many and his men would soon be overwhelmed.

Frustrated at missing the Roman with his first thrust, the large Armenian tried to reach over and stab down at Corvo, but in doing so he exposed himself far too much and the legionary behind Corvo thrust his own gladius forward, catching the Armenian in the throat. Corvo then smashed his shield forward, striking the man in the chest and sending him sprawling backwards, taking two of his comrades with him. Corvo retook his position in the line, risking a quick glance behind to see who had helped him despatch the big Armenian. He was surprised to see Faustus, looking grim.

Corvo nodded his gratitude as he felt another sword slam into his shield. Corvo flicked his own gladius out and caught the man on his shoulder. It was not a killing blow, but it was enough to send the man howling from the fight, at least for now.

An arrow thudded into his shield, quickly followed by another. It appeared to Corvo that although he wasn't wearing any insignia or uniform, the Armenians had somehow worked out he was the leader and had targeted him. To the rear of the fighting he briefly caught sight of the Armenian guard from the bridge he had spared and then questioned. In the surprise attack, the man had managed to escape to his comrades and was now directing the archers as to who to shoot at. Perhaps Drax had been right all along, and they should have killed him straight away.

Corvo thrust his gladius out at the exposed neck of another warrior, but this one had quicker reflexes and the man raised his shield to deflect the blow. He immediately made a thrust of his own, but there was no way past Corvo's shield. Suddenly lifting his own shield high, Corvo dropped low and thrust his gladius into the other man's groin. The Armenian screamed in agony, dropped his weapon and staggered back, crashing into his comrades as blood gushed down his thighs.

Corvo felt another arrow fly by his ear and heard the thud as it found a target. The man next to him collapsed to the ground, an arrow embedded in his left eye. The men behind him instantly hauled his body out of the way. Corvo glanced to his left and saw Faustus now standing in the line next to him.

"Keep your shield up and locked with mine and when I say push, push for all you're worth."

The young man nodded and did as instructed.

"Centurion! Centurion!" Atilus was calling him. "A fresh force of cavalry are arriving at the rear. Let my men at them."

This was not what Corvo wanted to hear. More cavalry and more archers. "Not yet, Atilus, they will cut your men down — " He stopped mid-sentence as he slammed his shield into the face of a snarling Armenian, shattering his nose before landing a powerful stroke from his gladius into the man's shoulder. It was such a strong blow that Corvo had trouble withdrawing his blade and in the end he had to kick the man's dying body away to free his weapon.

The Armenians pulled back a couple of paces, disengaging with the Romans. Some were glancing nervously over their shoulders towards the rear. Cries of alarm went up as panic swept through the Armenian ranks. Corvo was confused. His men were holding the Armenians back, but they would soon have to retreat or be overwhelmed, especially with the arrival of another wave of cavalry. Why, then, were the Armenians starting to withdraw instead of pressing home the attack?

"What's happening, Centurion?" asked Faustus. "Why do they no longer attack?"

"Damned if I know."

"Corvo, press home the attack!" shouted Arus, forcing his way through what remained of the second rank so that Corvo could hear him.

"But they've got reinforcements."

"They're friends."

"They're what?" shouted Corvo, bewildered.

"Friends. Our allies. Press the attack. Finish them!" roared Arus.

"Atilus, now is your time!" shouted Corvo. Atilus didn't hesitate. The small band of gladiators pushed their way through the depleted Roman ranks and tore into the confused Armenians, slashing and cutting enemy soldiers down as if they were nothing more than wheat in a field.

"The rest of you, forward on me, and keep those lines tight," called Corvo. Slowly, with shields locked and gladii poised to strike from above, the Romans began to advance. Any men that managed to avoid Atilus and his ruthless killers would now find themselves assailed by two lines of Roman steel, a killing formation that was hard to overcome. Trapped between Corvo and his men at one end of the bridge and whoever these mystery riders were behind, there was nowhere for the Armenians to go. Some continued to fight, but were quickly cut down as the vice closed around them. Some tried to escape by jumping into the river below, only to be picked off by Flavius' and the Syrians' arrows. The Armenians quickly realised the hopelessness of their situation and began to drop their weapons, but it was not enough to save them. Corvo looked on in dismay as the now unarmed Armenians were cut down by Drax and some of the others, aided by the newcomers. Corvo halted his men and waited for the killing to subside. The butchery was soon over.

One of the horsemen who had suddenly appeared behind the Armenians, dismounted and started to pick his way through the bodies towards the Romans. Arus strode out to meet him. The horseman was tall and well-built and towered over Arus by some inches. They exchanged words Corvo couldn't hear, and the stranger bowed to Arus. Then the two men clasped arms. Arus turned and looked at Corvo before leading the other man to him.

"Narek, this is Centurion Corvo who commands these men. Centurion, this is Narek of the Wahidi clan … our allies."

"Armenians?" asked Corvo.

"Armenians. Narek and his people have no love for the Parthians or their Armenian puppet king. They fight with us against our enemies."

Corvo nodded at Narek, who again offered a shallow bow.

"Your arrival was most fortuitous, Narek. You have my gratitude," said Corvo.

"Not fortuitous, Centurion, but pre-arranged," replied the Armenian.

"Oh?"

"We have been waiting here for some days. You are late."

"Apologies. Had I known we had allies waiting to help us, I would perhaps have driven the men harder." Corvo glared at Arus.

"There was no need for you to know, Centurion," said Arus.

Corvo wasn't convinced, but this was not the time for an argument.

"So these men are from Vermuk?" asked Corvo.

"They are," replied Narek.

"Then they will be missed, surely? Relief guards will be sent?"

"These men —" Narek waved his hand around at the dead lying all about them — "are their relief. They are responsible for guarding the bridge and patrolling this area. Eventually another force will come and relieve them, but that will not be for some days, and by then we will be far away."

"Or dead," said Corvo.

"In either case it will not matter. Until then my men will take turns to guard the bridge in case any other collaborators turn up. Tomorrow, we free your friends."

"Where do we hide until then?"

"You are all to be guests at my camp. It is not much but we have wine, food and fires. Your men can rest whilst we plan our attack."

"What about them?" It was Corvo's turn to point at the dead.

"We will take them into the forest. They will not be found there — not until we are long gone, anyway. Now come, let's set about our work so we can return to my camp." Narek gave some rapid orders, and his men immediately began the arduous job of picking up the bodies and slinging them across the horses' backs. Others would have to be carried, and Corvo issued orders for his men to help. This was met with groans until Galba told them there was wine and food waiting for them once the job was done.

Even with the combined force of Romans and Armenians, it took the best part of two hours to clear the bridge and surrounding area of bodies and weapons. By the time they had finished, a casual traveller would be hard put to realise that a skirmish had taken place there. After posting six of his men as guards, Narek led the tired and hungry men back to his camp inside the forest.

Corvo was amazed at the size of the camp and how it had so far avoided detection by Armenian forces loyal to Parthia. Narek laughed, saying that the Armenians and their Parthian puppet masters were afraid of the forest, believing imps and demons inhabited it. This belief had been fermented by the fact that whenever his men captured an enemy soldier or collaborator, they strung up their bodies in the trees for passers-by to see. When they returned to the neighbouring towns and villages, those travellers spoke of bodies torn apart by demons and the myth spiralled from there.

Narek had been true to his word and the few women who lived in the camp had obviously been busy preparing a meal for their menfolk and their Roman guests. The aromas coming from some of the campfires were almost too much for the men to bear. Others were hungry for something else and eyed the women lasciviously, which did not go unnoticed by Corvo.

"Lucius, before we dismiss the men to eat and rest, tell them that we are guests here and they will act accordingly. Any man who causes trouble, be it fighting, stealing or abusing the women, will be dealt with severely. Remind them what happened to Livius Camillus."

Flavius nodded.

"I should not worry too much, Centurion," said Narek, who had overheard what Corvo had said. "Our women can be even more fierce than our warriors when they have a mind to be and can look after themselves."

"That is good to know, Narek. Nevertheless, I don't want any discord between our men the night before the conclusion of our mission."

"As you wish, Centurion. Now come, let us eat and drink as friends and allies at my fire, for this time tomorrow we may be nothing but carrion." He strode away towards the centre of the camp, where several carcasses were being turned on spits.

"Now there's a comforting thought," said Flavius, grinning. He turned to face their men, traipsing into camp behind them. Bellowing for them to form three ranks, he waited patiently as Galba and Nerva cajoled them into position. The men were tired, hungry and irritable, and Corvo's warning about behaving in their hosts' camp was received as warmly as he expected. The grumbling soon died down, however, when Flavius mentioned Camillus. They all remembered that Corvo had hung the man himself for desertion.

"Cheer up, men, there is plenty of food and wine, so go have your fill of both."

The soldiers cheered and then dispersed in a disorderly fashion, each keen to be the first to be fed.

The evening passed in good spirits and the Armenians proved to be generous and convivial hosts. Corvo's worries about his men proved to be largely unfounded. He was pleased to see that despite the fact that few of Narek's men spoke Latin and virtually none of his Armenian, the two groups were laughing and joking together as they all grew steadily drunker.

As the evening wore on, the camp grew noisier and Corvo began to fear that passing Armenian patrols might hear them. Narek again assured him that they were too far into the forest to be heard and that the Armenians rarely patrolled at night.

"What about the fires? Won't they see those and come to investigate?" he asked.

"We are too far in for them to see them, but even if they did, they would think it bandits or renegades or perhaps the evil spirits," laughed Narek. When the Roman officer didn't join in,

Narek sought to reassure him further. "Relax, Centurion. We have men on the bridge, and I have lookouts posted at the far end of the forest in the direction we will be heading tomorrow. If so much as a wolf moves, I will hear about it."

Hearing there were wolves in the forest did nothing to assuage Corvo's anxiety.

"Very well. Perhaps you can tell me what you know of Vermuk and its garrison?"

Narek was suddenly serious. "Vermuk is … what do you Romans say? Oh yes, Hades."

"So I keep hearing, but what I haven't heard is how we're going to gain entry and get our men out." Corvo looked from Narek to Arus. He didn't doubt that the two men had discussed and probably agreed a plan to breach the town. It made Corvo wonder just what else they had discussed. It also made him wonder why he was even there if decisions so critical to the mission had already been agreed upon.

Arus gestured for Narek to speak.

"Vermuk is a day's march from here. First through this forest, then across a valley at the top of which we will be able to see Vermuk. We will descend through a wooded slope and emerge onto a plain. From there it is two hours' march to the town walls."

"Two hours of open countryside! How in Jupiter's name are we to cross that without being seen?" Corvo's irritation was growing. If he had known about this in advance, it would have given him enough time to come up with a plan that gave them a better than zero chance of survival.

"We will rest here tomorrow and then travel at night. We will then spend the next day resting in the trees overlooking the plain leading to the town. Shortly after the darkest hour, we will cross the plain and gain access to the town. We will then find your friends and you can escape."

"Surely you mean *we* can escape?" said Corvo.

"This is my country, Centurion. I have nowhere to escape to."

"So what will you do?"

Narek and Arus exchanged a look Corvo didn't like.

"In exchange for his help, we are giving Narek and his men a free hand in the town to do as he pleases."

"Meaning?"

"Meaning my enemies within the town and those who have aided them will come to regret their actions. If there is enough support within the town for our cause, as I suspect there is, I will attempt to hold the town until our Roman allies return."

"With just these men? That's suicide, Narek," said Corvo.

"Suicide. Glory. It's all the same thing. Besides, if we are successful, word will spread and others will join us."

"So too will your enemy countrymen. Or the Parthians."

"Let them. They will not get into the town easily."

"Which brings me to my next question. How will *we* get into the town?"

"I have men on the inside. They will kill the guards and open the gate after signalling to us that the way is clear."

"You make it sound simple, Narek," said Corvo.

"And so it should be … in theory. But I caution you now, both of you —" he glanced at Arus — "the man who commands Vermuk is a brute. Your men will not be in great shape."

"But your men have confirmed that they are alive?"

"The last I heard, not three days ago, they yet draw breath."

“Our plan is to take the whole town, Corvo,” said Arus. “But if that proves impossible, I must remind you that our mission is to rescue the tribune, not his men.”

“Then let us hope that your plan works, and we are able to take the town. Now, it is about time you shared with Lucius, Titus and I just what this plan is.”

Arus nodded and whilst he went to find Flavius and drag Galba away from an arm-wrestling contest, Narek called for more wine. Then, when everybody was seated again and their cups full, Arus began to talk.

CHAPTER 13

They had talked long into the night, safe in the knowledge that the hours of sleep they were losing could be caught up on the next day. The plan Arus had constructed was a good one, but he was not a soldier, and both Corvo and Galba had suggested revisions. By the time they finally retired to their sleeping blankets, a plan that was acceptable to them all had been agreed upon.

There were still too many variables for Corvo's liking — was the garrison only a hundred and fifty men strong like Narek seemed to believe, or was it nearer three hundred, as their former prisoner had claimed? How far away were their nearest reinforcements, or had they just wiped those out on the bridge? Were Narek's men on the inside of the town still free, or had they been discovered? These and other fears raced through his mind as he lay down, but a combination of exhaustion from the fight and a healthy amount of wine soon saw him fall into a deep sleep.

Corvo woke shortly after dawn to find the camp bustling with activity, though when he finally managed to sit up he saw that most of those hurrying about the camp were Armenian women preparing food and some of their men tending to the few animals kept within pens inside the small camp. The handful of Corvo's men moving about the place did so sluggishly and with sour looks on their faces.

Corvo sensed movement beside him and turned gingerly to see Flavius wincing as he moved into a sitting position.

"For the love of the gods, they must have poisoned us," exclaimed Flavius, grasping the sides of his head with both hands. "My head feels like Mars' war chariot is thundering around inside."

"I think this may be the real reason why we are moving tonight and not today," replied Corvo.

"Well, I for one would rather face a quick death from an Armenian sword or Parthian arrow than a lingering death from this headache." He made to lie down again, but Corvo reached over and grasped his arm.

"I wouldn't do that if I were you. I've tried it, and it doesn't help."

"Then just leave me here to die."

"Good morning, Centurion, Lucius."

"Titus! How are you standing?" asked Corvo. "I saw you drink far more than us."

"What, that watered-down horse piss? My grandmother could have handled that. They must have kept the good stuff hidden."

"Greetings, friends," said Narek, beaming as he emerged from a nearby tent.

"Greetings, Narek. We were just discussing your wine."

"Enjoyable, is it not?"

"I can't deny that, but perhaps a warning that it was likely to decimate my force would not have gone amiss," said Corvo plaintively.

Narek laughed heartily. "I have never seen an outsider consume as much as Titus here and still live. Are you sure you're not Armenian, my friend?"

Galba beat a closed fist to his chest. "I am Roman through and through."

"Then we must make you an honorary member of my clan; the ceremony will involve much drinking."

Corvo and Flavius both paled at the thought, making Narek laugh again.

"But perhaps we will wait until our little adventure is over."

"Yes, let's do that," said Flavius, grimacing.

"Come, my friends, let's eat," said Narek. "We will all need our strength over the next few days."

"Now that's the best thing you've said so far," said Galba. "Then you can show me where you keep the good stuff."

Narek laughed again and slapped Galba on the back. "Maybe, my friend, maybe."

After they had eaten, Nerva had suggested taking the men on a brief march through the forest to shake off any lingering aftereffects of the wine, but Corvo had denied him, claiming the men could use the rest. Nerva himself had seemed relieved. Instead, Corvo had insisted on a brief parade, where a roll call was carried out, and the men were instructed to check their weapons, rest and conserve their strength.

The day passed in good spirits, with most of Corvo's men spending the time checking and cleaning their kit, gambling or sleeping. By the evening meal, the men's spirits seemed restored and Corvo was greeted warmly by the clusters of men gathered around the camp. Corvo's confidence was also restored, and he began to wonder if perhaps they really could pull this rescue mission off.

The hours dragged and while Corvo was eager to get going, Narek assured him that they had plenty of time. So long as they reached the woods at the foot of the valley by dawn, all would be well. There they would rest for the entirety of the next day, before crossing the plain and commencing their assault.

As they made what actually turned out to be a straightforward journey, Narek had to encourage Corvo to slow down from the forced march pace he was setting for his men. The Armenians, sitting upon their horses, watched in amusement. They arrived at the top of the slope that led down to the plain a couple of hours before first light, giving Corvo and his men a brief glimpse of the distant town of Vermuk. Then Narek led them down the slope and deep into the trees before signalling for the men to halt.

"We will camp here for the day. There must be no fires and noise must be kept to a minimum. I will post men to watch our rear if you can set guards to watch over the plain towards the town, Centurion?"

Corvo nodded and gestured for Galba to arrange it.

"We are here at last, Centurion," said Arus.

"Indeed. It has been a long road from Rome."

"Let us hope that there is a reward at the end then."

"Have we missed anything, Arus?"

"You have doubts?"

"I would not be a good officer if I did not. In my experience a complacent officer in the morning is usually a dead officer by the evening."

Arus laughed. "You could be right. But I believe we have the best plan possible given our limited resources. Of course I'd rather be standing here amongst a full-strength legion with ballistae to our rear, but we must make do with what we have. The gods will either smile on us or they will turn their backs. There is little us mortals can do about that."

"I didn't think a man in your role would give so much credence to the gods."

"I don't, but it doesn't hurt to have a back-up plan, does it?" Arus smiled. "Rest, Centurion, and tonight we shall find out if our preparations were enough. There is no turning back now. We either succeed or we die."

Corvo nodded. He suspected that it was going to be a long day.

As it started to get dark, Corvo decided it was time to bring the men under his command up to speed on their mission and what was expected of them.

Galba and Nerva had mustered the men into three ranks in the only bit of space that could accommodate them near their camp, and Corvo now paced up and down in front of them. Finally he came to a stop and stepped up onto a log that Galba had thoughtfully placed there for him. It wasn't that he was smaller than some of the men, just that he wanted to be able to see everyone's faces, and they his.

"It has been a long journey from Rome, men. A long and arduous journey with many obstacles along the way, but we have dealt with them all."

"None of them were as bad as Narek's wine, sir," called a voice from the second line.

"Quiet in the ranks!" shouted Nerva, eyeing the men and trying to identify the joker.

Corvo signalled for Nerva to relax. "No, you are right, none as lethal as that. Now we face our greatest challenge, the reason we put this force together in the first place." Corvo could sense the air of anticipation as the men strained to hear the reason they had been marched halfway across the known world. "In a few hours' time, we will leave the majority of our equipment here, descend the slope and emerge onto a plain some of you may have seen when we breasted the valley earlier. Some of you may also have seen the town of Vermuk in the distance." A few of the men nodded. "We will cross that plain and arrive just outside the town walls, a couple of hours after the darkest hour. As I have told you before, inside that town a number of our brother soldiers are being held captive by the Armenians. One of those captives is a legate's son. We are going to enter the town, free the captives and, if possible, take the town. After that we will make a run for Syria, leaving Narek and his men to hold the town until our legions relieve them." The men broke into animated discussion and Nerva glanced at Corvo. Corvo shook his head and instead waited patiently for the hubbub to die down, which it did a short while later.

"How do we gain entry to the town, sir?" asked Traianus.

"Narek has men on the inside who will eliminate the guards and then open the gates. Narek and his men will race in, and we will follow as quickly as possible. There is to be no murder of civilians unless you or your comrades are threatened. Whatever plunder you find is yours." There was more animated chatter, which Corvo quashed with a silencing hand gesture.

"And the enemy, sir?" asked another soldier.

"They are all to be killed. If we are to escape and make it safely back to our own lines, we need a good head start, and leaving enemy soldiers alive who may raise the alarm is not a risk we can afford to take."

"Why not just wait with Narek and his men for the legions to come and relieve us? We're safer here behind walls, surely?" asked Decimus, the former gladiator.

"Because there is no guarantee the legions will come. At least not for some time." Corvo studied the faces of his men and decided to answer the unasked question. "Narek and his men know there are no guarantees, but this is their country, and they are prepared to fight and die for it if necessary." Some of the men glanced over at Narek's men, who were huddled around their leader, no doubt being given much the same speech. Corvo glanced at the darkening sky. "It won't be long until we leave, so use the remaining time wisely. Carry only what you need: weapons and food and water to be consumed on the way. Remove anything that might jangle or make a noise. The plain is either sandy or hardpacked, so tread carefully. If we win, there will be wine and water aplenty. If we lose … well, you won't be needing a drink if your head's no longer attached to your neck." The men laughed. "Fight well, fight for Rome, and fight for the man beside you. When this is over, mention of the 'Legion of The Damned' will send chills down our enemy's spines. Dismissed."

It seemed the gods were with the Romans. Not long before they formed up to leave the camp and descend the slope out onto the plain, the sky had started to darken, the moon disappearing behind the clouds. By the time they emerged from the trees onto the plain, the moonlight had vanished.

The Armenians had swaddled their horses' hooves in rags and gently walked them alongside their Roman allies towards a gulley Narek assured them existed no more than half a mile from the town's gates. Once there, they would lie low and await the signal from the Armenian guards on the ramparts.

The men had all prepared well and unless the enemy knew they were there, it would be hard to tell that almost a hundred men and forty horses were traipsing across the plain.

The temptation to move faster and make the most of the darkness was almost overpowering, but Corvo knew that if he pushed the men then mistakes could be made. It would only take one small sound to give them away. They would then either be cut down in the open, or left to die of thirst outside a town fully alert and on guard against their attack. Remaining hidden in the gulley for longer than anticipated could also lead to problems, especially for Narek's men, who needed to not only ensure their own silence, but that of their mounts too. Corvo wanted his men calm and focused when they entered the town. The odds against them were already too great to risk otherwise.

It was with relief that Corvo eventually arrived at the gulley and began dispersing his men, especially as the gods had apparently chosen to withdraw their favour and the skies were once again clearing, leaving the plains bathed in a pale, silvery light. Corvo waited for any indication that their presence had been noticed. No cries of alarm were heard, yet Corvo still worried. What if they had seen them and were now busily filling the ramparts with archers who would slaughter his men out in the open? Narek's men would not be able to send the signal and the attack could not go ahead as planned. How would they then withdraw? Corvo wiped his palms on his tunic.

"That went surprisingly well," whispered Flavius, moving up alongside Corvo.

"Our cover has gone, though," said Corvo bitterly, glancing up at the sky.

"True, but if Narek's men inside do their job well, then that won't matter as there will be nobody on the ramparts to spot us. If they don't — well, I suppose it won't matter a great deal anyway."

Corvo lay back against the slope, his back to the town. The worst thing about any fight was the waiting. To his left his men fanned out, lying against the reverse slope as he was. To his right were more of his men and beyond them, Narek and his men lay soothing and whispering to their horses. Corvo briefly locked eyes with Narek and nodded. The Armenian smiled back.

Time crawled by and with each passing minute Corvo's anxiety grew, certain that they would soon be discovered. Then Flavius shook his shoulder and pointed to the distant walls of the town. There, high on the ramparts, a lone figure was waving a lit torch back and forth.

It was time.

CHAPTER 14

Corvo turned to tell Narek, but he had already seen the signal. His men coaxed their horses to stand before quickly mounting them. Narek gave a hand signal, and his men eased their horses up the ridge and onto the plain. When everyone was up, another signal was given, and the Armenians began to trot towards the town. When they were no more than four hundred paces away, Narek drew his sword and gave the signal to charge. His men drew their own weapons and crouched low over their horses, urging them ever faster towards the gates which, as they drew nearer, began to swing open.

As soon as Narek and his men had cleared the gulley, Corvo gave the signal for his own men to rise and they quickly formed up in two lines. After checking that nobody had been left behind, Corvo gave the signal to advance. They walked briskly at first, then when Corvo raised his gladius into the air they began to jog. When Corvo lowered it to point at the town, the men charged forward.

Unencumbered by their usual armour and kit, the men were able to move quickly, and they covered the ground in no time. Atilus and his gladiators led the way, though a few of the legionaries tried to match their pace. They were no more than eighty strides from the town gates when the first sounds of battle reached Corvo's ears.

By the time Corvo passed through the town gates, chaos ruled. Most of Narek's men had dismounted and were engaging with the few Armenian soldiers who had managed to grab their weapons and come out onto the streets to confront the invaders. A few of Narek's men had remained on their horses and together with the two Syrians who had ridden in with them, now fired arrows at the enemy warriors as they emerged bleary-eyed from their barracks. Their surprise attack had worked and for the moment Corvo and his men had the advantage, but he knew that shortly the sheer weight of numbers would swing the battle in the defenders' favour. Already Corvo could see clusters of Armenians organising themselves, and archers were being deployed to the ramparts.

Corvo's men fanned out around him, all except Arus, Brutus, Nerva and Faustus, who remained at Corvo's side. In the town square the former gladiators had torn into the defenders with a wild abandon that made Corvo wince. Their recklessness went against everything he had ever been told or trained to do. He fought back the instinct to call them back to reorganise; the gladiators only knew how to fight one way and that was with aggression and speed. Corvo had to admit that whilst it wasn't pretty to watch, it was highly effective as they carved a swathe through the enemy, who had never before encountered such wild aggression. There was only one thing they could do, and Corvo watched in horror as the Armenian archers turned their bows on the gladiators. Moments later, Decimus' body rocked as three arrows struck him, one in the thigh, one in the side and the third straight through his right hand, causing him to drop his gladius.

Decimus looked down at the arrows piercing his body and then up at the ramparts from where the arrows had been fired. Seemingly oblivious to the pain, he bent over and picked up his gladius with his left hand. As he straightened up, another two arrows struck him, one in the chest and one in the throat. Still clutching his gladius, he collapsed to the ground.

"We've got to clear those archers off the ramparts," Corvo said, turning to face the cluster of men with him. "You up for a fight, Arus?"

"I thought you'd never ask."

"Then on me, all of you." Corvo raced towards the nearest steps, closely followed by the others. Their approach had been noticed and two of the bowmen were now pointing their bows towards Corvo and the others.

"Shields!" yelled Corvo as he pulled Arus down behind him. Moments later an arrow thumped into his own shield. "Forward," he urged as they raced up the steps. Corvo knew they would never reach the bowmen before they managed to loose off more arrows, but they had no choice but to keep going. Corvo was the first to reach the ramparts and just had time to raise his shield before another arrow thudded into it.

Discarding his shield, Corvo was up and racing towards the two archers. One of the archers managed to nock another arrow, but before he had a chance to fire, a javelin struck him in the back. It had been hurled with such force that the tip emerged from the man's stomach. The second archer didn't have time to take in what had happened to his comrade before Corvo had thrust his gladius clean through his chest. Corvo quickly tipped both bodies over the side and down onto the ground below. He cast a glance round to see who had thrown the javelin, but whoever it was had moved on and taken up another fight elsewhere.

The three remaining archers on the rampart were now engaged in a firing contest with the two Syrian brothers. Now and again one of the Armenians would stop and take a shot at the Romans below, but it was now too compact with opposing troops to risk firing and hitting one of their own.

When the two Syrians saw Corvo and the others approaching the bowmen, they turned away to select new targets and by the time the Armenians realised the danger they were in, it was already too late. Corvo sliced his gladius across the neck of one of the bowmen with such force that the man's head was partially severed. Another bowman dropped his bow and drew a short sword, but before he could ready himself, Arus had lunged forward and stabbed the man in the stomach. The two men locked eyes before Arus pulled his gladius free, blood and entrails spilling out onto the rampart. The bowman fell backwards over the rampart, crushing one of his comrades on the ground below.

The last bowman had thrown down his weapon and fled along the ramparts. He ran into a group of his comrades coming the opposite way, but instead of finding safety with them, he was roughly shoved off the ramparts by the group's leader, who was clearly disgusted by his cowardice. These men were going to be a different proposition, Corvo realised.

The two groups of men stared at each other, and then, bellowing a challenge, they charged. The rampart wasn't wide enough for everyone to engage an enemy, so the first to lock weapons were Corvo and Nerva. Corvo was relieved to find that he had an experienced legionary next to him, watching his flank. Arus was an old man by comparison, more used to scheming than fighting, though there was no doubting his courage. Faustus was an unknown entity, though he had acquitted himself well in the hills.

The Armenian leader had identified Corvo as the Roman leader and immediately engaged him. He was a big man, with jet-black hair and a neat, oiled beard. He was clearly no stranger to combat, and a series of quick sword strokes soon had Corvo moving backwards. Nerva was not faring much better, and to avoid becoming isolated a couple of paces ahead of Corvo and potentially being flanked, he had allowed himself to be driven back at the same pace as Corvo.

Both Armenians were excellent swordsmen and Corvo silently cursed himself for discarding his shield. The big Armenian continued to drive Corvo back, but his swings and thrusts were reducing in speed and intensity as he tired. Corvo knew that if he just remained patient, an opportunity would present itself.

To his left, Nerva appeared to be getting the upper hand with his opponent and was slowly pushing him backwards. The Armenian facing Corvo suddenly changed tack and instead of trying to thrust at Corvo, he now delivered a powerful slice which only narrowly missed the top of his head. Sensing that this was his chance, Corvo thrust his gladius forward, hoping to catch the man off-balance, but the Armenian twisted sideways just in time to avoid the full force of the thrust, though it did leave him with a gash.

Nerva had finally overpowered his adversary, who had been stabbed deeply in the side. Whilst it was not a killing blow, it was enough to send the man sprawling to the rampart floor. His fall, together with his cry of alarm, was enough to momentarily distract the warrior facing Corvo, who seized his chance. He launched a series of powerful downward slashes at his opponent, the ferocity of which was enough to drive him back.

Then the Fates smiled on Corvo. One of the Syrians in the courtyard below saw an opportunity and fired an arrow at the cluster of men behind Corvo's adversary. The arrow went clean through the neck of the man standing directly behind the big Armenian and he immediately collapsed to the ground, dead. Corvo's opponent took one pace back, readying himself to launch at Corvo, but instead he tripped over the body lying behind him and stumbled backwards. Corvo was on him in a flash. He thrust his gladius into the man's heart, killing him instantly.

Now outnumbered two against four, the remaining Armenians began to slowly back away, but Corvo and Nerva weren't about to let that happen and, scrambling over the bodies of their dead comrades, they pressed home their attack. Both men were soon overpowered and despatched.

"The ramparts are ours, Centurion," said Nerva, breathing heavily.

Corvo looked around and saw that it was true. Atilus and some of his men had mounted and cleared the western rampart; the broken and bloodied Armenian bodies lying on the ground beneath it were a testament to the savagery of their attack. Below him, in the town square, Flavius and Galba had formed two lines of legionaries and were simultaneously driving the enemy back towards each other. The Armenians would be caught between the two walls of steel and mercilessly slaughtered. Elsewhere around the square and nearby streets, the rest of Corvo's men and all of Narek's men were involved in a series of melees with the defenders. The skirmishes between Narek's men and the defending Armenians seemed particularly brutal as each saw the other as a traitor to their country.

Corvo was impressed by Narek's fighting capabilities as he was confronted by three of his fellow countrymen. Killing Narek would make them heroes, and so they went about their task with a grim determination. But Narek was not for running. In fact, such was the ferocity of his onslaught that they were immediately on the back foot, and Corvo watched as one was despatched with a neat thrust to the stomach whilst another received a deep cut to his sword arm, severing the tendon and forcing the man to drop his weapon and turn away, howling in pain.

"Centurion, we need to find the tribune," said Arus.

"Yes, of course," replied Corvo. "There is no escape. That is the only gate, and our men have barred it and stand guard. But I agree we need to find the prisoners in case they try to use them as bargaining chips."

"I don't think Narek is the sort to make deals," said Arus, watching something behind Corvo.

Corvo turned and saw that Narek had driven his last opponent to his knees. With a powerful thrust, Narek drove his sword into the man's open mouth with such force, that the tip emerged out of the back of the man's head. Pushing the man's body backwards with his foot, Narek hurried on down the street to where two of his men appeared hard-pressed by a cluster of enemy warriors. Corvo suspected that the odds had just swung monumentally in the attackers' favour.

"I see what you mean," replied Corvo. "Sextus, gather some men and hold these ramparts. Relieve Atilus and his men too; they will be of more use in the streets. Post the Syrians up here for cover." Nerva nodded and was already barking orders at men before he had descended the steps. Within a very short space of time all the ramparts were manned by Corvo's men, with the two Syrian archers stationed on either rampart. Not for the first time Corvo wished that he had recruited more men proficient with a bow.

"Right, let's find these prisoners," said Corvo, satisfied at the deployments. He started down the steps, followed by Arus and Faustus.

The three men picked their way across the dead and the dying in the square. Corvo stopped briefly when an arm suddenly reached up towards him. He knelt down and clasped the hand of the man he recognised as Aquilanus, one of the handful of regular legionaries he had been allowed to recruit.

"Did we win, Centurion?" the man asked in a faltering voice, blood seeping from the corner of his mouth.

"Thanks to the bravery of men like you, Aquilanus, we will carry this day. You fought well; I was watching from the ramparts." It was a lie. Corvo had not seen Aquilanus fight, but there was no harm in giving the man some comfort in his final moments. The fallen legionary tried to smile, but it just made him choke, thick red blood splattering his chin and tunic. Corvo felt the man's grip on his hand loosen and watched as the light in his eyes faded. His spirit had left for Elysium. Corvo gently laid the legionary's hand on his chest. Then, spying Aquilanus' gladius lying nearby, he carefully slipped it into the man's dead grasp.

"Rest easy, soldier of Rome." Corvo stood and hurried towards the centre of the town.

CHAPTER 15

The air was full of screams and the clash of metal.

Corvo, Arus and Faustus hurried through the town towards where Arus had been told the captives were being held, avoiding fights where possible. Corvo had no idea how many Armenians would be guarding the prisoners and didn't want to find himself confronted by a band of enemy warriors with just an old man and untried youngster as his support.

Much of the fighting was over now, at least on this side of the town. Now was the time for vengeance. Narek's troops felled every man and boy of fighting age they found. Corvo understood that this was the way of conquering armies; he had seen his own comrades do it often enough when they took a village or camp. He also understood he was powerless to stop it.

"There!" said Arus, pointing to a building as they rounded a corner.

Corvo signalled for them to stop and edged back around the corner, out of sight. Neither guard stationed outside the building had caught sight of them. They had both been staring down the main thoroughfare, expecting any attackers to come from that direction, whereas Arus had led them through the backstreets. How he had known which way to go was a mystery to Corvo.

"How many?" asked Arus.

"Two guards," said Corvo. "They don't appear to have seen us. There is sure to be more inside."

"So what's the plan?"

Corvo wiped the sweat from his forehead with the back of his hand as he considered their next move. If they charged at them, the guards would simply disappear inside and bolt the doors. Taking the building then would be a difficult business. In all likelihood, whoever commanded inside the building would have the prisoners killed, or bargain their lives in return for safe passage out of the town. Whilst Corvo would be prepared to bargain, Narek most certainly would not, and he couldn't afford a split with their newfound allies.

He explained his thoughts to Arus, and the other man rubbed his bristly chin as he considered the problem. "What if just one or two men approach? The guards may be inclined to stay in position and guard the door if they feel less threatened. Once they're engaged, the rest of us could flank them and cut off their retreat to the door, thereby securing our entry point."

Arus' plan had merit, but it was far from foolproof. For a start there was only the three of them, though Corvo had no doubt others would soon appear. Having no better suggestions himself and with time running out, Corvo knew he had to act.

"I'll go," he said.

Arus shook his head. "That's not a good idea, Centurion. If we lose you…"

"Optio Flavius is a fine officer and Galba is more than capable. He is far more experienced than me and ought to be leading this mission anyway."

"Perhaps, but he isn't — you are."

"Today is not my day to die, Arus," Corvo assured him with a grin. He risked a quick peek around the corner and saw that both of the guards had stepped forward from their position at the door. Although the sounds of battle had largely receded now, the odd clash of steel could still be heard. Something had clearly drawn their attention, and it increased the likelihood of them engaging Corvo when he showed himself. Adjusting his grip on his gladius, Corvo readied himself to race forward. At that moment a familiar sound reached his ears, and he carefully poked his head round the corner for another look.

Corvo watched as a dozen or so javelins arced through the air and began their descent of death. Both of the guards had seen them, and one turned to run whilst his comrade froze, as if transfixed. Moments later most of the javelins thudded harmlessly into the sand, but three had found their targets. Two of the javelins had pierced the man who had turned to run, their points travelling through his flesh to bury themselves in the sand in front of him, pinning him to the ground. His comrade had been struck through the thigh and was now lying on the sand, screaming in pain.

"He is going to alert those inside to our presence," warned Arus.

Corvo raced across the distance to where the man lay wailing and quickly slit his throat to silence him. Behind him, Corvo heard the sound of men approaching.

He turned to see Flavius leading a score of soldiers, Atilus and three of his gladiators amongst their number.

"Well met, Lucius."

"You too, brother," replied Flavius, clasping his friend's arm in the traditional warrior's embrace.

Arus and Faustus, meanwhile, had crossed the clearing to join them. Corvo now estimated that he had about twenty-five swords with him.

"How goes the battle?" asked Corvo.

"The town is all but ours. Sextus and some men hold all of the ramparts, and Titus is clearing out any last resistance. We caught most of their men in a vice in the square and destroyed them."

"Well done," said Corvo, slapping his friend on the shoulder. As he did so, he noticed a frown cross his friend's face. "What is it, Lucius?"

"Narek's men … they're killing everyone they find. None are spared."

"I know. I witnessed some of it on my way here. There is nothing we can do, Lucius. It is war. We must focus on the job we came here to do, and that's to rescue the tribune."

"What's the plan, Centurion?" asked Atilus.

"We believe the prisoners are being held in there," said Corvo, pointing to the building behind him. "We don't know how many of our men are still alive and we don't know how many men are guarding them."

"There will be no room for your men and their pretty lines inside. I will take my men in and we will clear the building," said Atilus confidently.

"It was our pretty lines that crushed the majority of the enemy in the town square, or have you forgotten?" said Flavius coldly. His usual jovial mood had long since departed.

"And perhaps you have forgotten that it was me and my men who stormed the town first and bought you time to get organised? Two of my brothers lie dead as a result," retorted Atilus.

"Everyone has played their part," said Corvo, trying to placate both men.

"Perhaps not everyone," said Atilus. He reached over and grabbed Faustus' wrist, raising his arm. The young man's gladius blade was as clean as it had been before the assault and as Corvo stared at it, he realised that he hadn't seen Faustus fight anyone, let alone kill; he had always been behind Corvo.

Faustus flushed under the intense gaze of those around him as Atilus let go of his wrist.

"Let us stay focused on the job at hand, shall we?" suggested Arus.

"Atilus and his men will follow me in," said Corvo. "Lucius, pick six men to remain out here in case any try to escape or reinforcements show up. Then follow me in with everyone else."

Just then the air was filled with shouting, and they all turned to see a score of Armenians enter the street, glancing nervously back in the direction from which they had come. A moment later, Narek and some of his men also came sprinting into the street, howling and roaring. For a moment it looked as if they had mistaken Corvo and his men for their quarry, and started to run towards them, but once they saw the blond hair of some of the men, they changed direction and raced down the street after the Armenians.

"I guess we don't have to worry about a counterattack from that direction now," said Corvo. "Still, leave six men out here and tell them to be vigilant, Lucius."

Flavius nodded and Corvo looked at Atilus.

"Are you ready?"

Atilus grinned. "Always."

Corvo borrowed a shield from one of the men and then turned and grasped the iron door ring and twisted it. The door opened easily and quietly, and then it gave off a squeal loud enough to wake the dead of Tartarus. Corvo cursed. If he had hoped to gain access to the building secretly, that possibility had passed, though he doubted that their arrival outside had gone unnoticed.

He pushed the door open and let the sunlight flood in. Dust motes danced in the air before him as he raised his shield and entered the building. There was little natural light in the first room they entered and just as Corvo's eyes began to adjust to the gloom, he felt a thud against his shield and then heard a gurgling sound coming from behind him. Bowmen were waiting for them inside.

Corvo raised his shield and stepped in front of the men standing behind him. "Out, get out!" he shouted as he started to back out of the door. His shield shook as two more arrows thudded into it from close range, the point of one emerging through the shield and missing Corvo's face by a fraction. He increased his pace backwards until he finally emerged back into the sunlight. He moved to the side of the door, which they had left open. One of Atilus' men had been struck in the throat and now lay dead on the ground beside the entrance.

Corvo cursed again. He should have anticipated the bowmen; now his negligence had cost him another soldier.

"New plan. You three with me," said Corvo, pointing to three men carrying shields. Turning to Atilus, he added, "We'll go in one at a time and link up to form a shield wall. As soon as we're done, you and your men come in behind us, but keep low. We'll then advance slowly until we're just a few paces away, then we'll break formation and you and your men rush the bowmen. Understood?"

"Understood."

"I'll go first, then you three in turn," said Corvo, pointing to the three legionaries. "Come in low with your shield up. Once we're in position, do not move until I give the command. Lucius, if one of us should fall before the wall is built, send another man in immediately." The men all nodded.

Corvo adjusted his grip and crouched low behind his shield. On entering the building, two more arrows immediately thumped into his protection, and he began to wonder how much longer it would hold. He took up a crouched position and as he did so, he heard the shuffling footfall of another man entering the building behind him. A moment later he felt the man's shield overlap his own. A few heartbeats later a second man joined their formation. Finally the third man carefully picked his way across the floor, locking shields with the man to his left. Satisfied that they were as secure as possible, Corvo called to Atilus and moments later, Atilus and Drax were crouched behind them. Arrows continued to pepper their protection, but the Romans had done their work well and no arrows found a gap.

"How many archers?" asked Atilus.

"Two, maybe three," replied Corvo.

"Then they are dead men — they just don't know it yet."

"On my mark we advance slowly, keeping the wall tight. At the word 'break' we will part the shields and you and Drax will need to rush forward and kill them before they can fire again." Atilus nodded and Corvo wondered if anything ever scared this former gladiator. "Shield wall, up." The men in line with Corvo stood as one. "Advance." The line began to walk steadily forward. Although the arrows continued to hit their shields, they were fewer than before. Either the Armenians were running out of arrows, or they had realised that the momentum was swinging in the Romans' favour, and they were now thinking about saving their own necks. If that was the case, they had left it too late. Corvo waited until he heard two arrows land in quick succession and then gave the order to break.

Atilus and Drax were on their feet before the shield wall parted. When it did, the former gladiators were through the gaps and racing towards the bowmen. The first fell to a slash across the chest from Atilus; the second nearly had his head removed by a powerful stroke from Drax's sword. The third bowman tried to flee but was too slow. Drax sliced the man across the back of his thighs, bringing him to the ground. After rolling the man over, the gladiator drove the point of his sword into the soft spot at the base of the man's throat.

Behind him, Corvo heard Flavius enter the building with the rest of the men, save for the ones ordered to remain on guard outside.

"Where now?" asked Flavius.

Corvo glanced around, his eyes now accustomed to the gloom. "There is only one way." He pointed at a solitary door.

"They'll be waiting for us, Marcus," whispered Flavius.

"I know. That's why I'm going first."

"Let some of the men take the risk. They're expendable; you're not."

"They may have been once, when we first set out, but not now. Now they're my men and I owe them my loyalty."

"If your loyalty stretches to men like Drax and Traianus, then I think you've taken one too many blows to the head. I'm not sure that they would return that loyalty."

"Nevertheless, I must lead by example."

"Let me and my men through. We will take the room for you," said Atilus, stepping forward. Drax roared his approval.

"If they've got more bowmen waiting inside, you'll be cut down in moments," said Corvo. "What use are you to me then?"

"Then what is your plan, Centurion?"

"I will go in first with my shield up, then Lucius and his men. Once we have established the shield wall, you —"

"I know. Come in low and quick," Atilus cut in.

Corvo gestured for his men to take up position on either side of the door, so that nobody got hit by projectiles once he swung it open. Hefting his shield into a more comfortable position and flexing his fingers around his gladius, he flung open the door and entered the room. It was large, with several large windows high up, allowing natural light in.

There was no thud of arrows this time. Instead, Corvo heard the roar of a warrior launching an attack and then the clatter of steel upon his shield.

Corvo parried a downward slash from a black-clad Armenian. The man was quick, and no sooner had Corvo blocked that swing than the attacker brought his weapon in low, trying to catch Corvo in the side. Corvo leapt back and managed to drop his sword in time to block the swipe. The next stroke was a backhanded slice, intended to open Corvo's stomach, but again he was equal to the man's attack. Both men backed off a pace or two, sizing each other up.

The respite over, the Armenian feinted to his right and then came in low. But Corvo had anticipated the move and deflected the man's blade. In doing so, the Armenian had made himself vulnerable on his right side. Corvo seized his moment. He slammed his shield into the side of the other man's head and then thrust his gladius into the man's right side. The Armenian cried out but didn't go down. Instead he launched a series of wild swipes at Corvo, all of which Corvo either deflected or ducked. An opportunity presented itself and Corvo slashed the man across the right calf. The Armenian collapsed to the ground in agony. Corvo was upon him in an instant and although the stricken man tried to ward him off with his sword, Corvo was soon able to disarm him. The Armenian warrior stared up in horror as Corvo hammered the edge of his shield down into the man's face. The Armenian stopped moving.

Corvo stepped back from the body and looked about him. The room was now full of his men, the enemy largely driven back to the end of the room, where they formed a defensive line. Bodies littered the floor. Corvo saw several of his men lying dead or wounded, but most of the bodies were dressed in black. He suspected that these were probably the commander of the town's personal bodyguard or his elite troops.

At the head of the throng were Atilus and Drax. They were covered in blood. The Armenian soldiers had been skilled warriors, but they had not been prepared for men like Atilus. Gladiators had their own unique way of fighting, a courage and recklessness that was foreign to a disciplined soldier. Clearly the Armenians had not been able to counter them, and had paid dearly for it in blood.

"Hold," commanded Corvo and as he did so, the Armenian line slowly parted. Behind them stood a man whom Corvo took to be the commander of the town. On his knees before him was a dirty and unkempt man, whose skin was as pale as moonlight, clearly having not seen sunlight for a long time. His hair was long and matted and his clothes nothing more than rags hanging from a thin frame. Even before the Armenian spoke, Corvo knew that this was Gaius, the tribune.

"One more step," said the commander in faltering Latin, "and your tribune dies." From the folds of his tunic the Armenian produced a dagger, which he held to the tribune's throat. "He is, after all, the reason you are here, is he not?"

"It's over, Donabedian. Let the tribune go," said Arus, pushing through Corvo's men to stand at the front, just a few paces from the Armenian soldiers.

Corvo and Atilus tensed, ready to rush forward if the Armenians attacked him.

"Who are you to speak my name?" said the town commander, glaring at Arus.

"I am Cornelius Arus, special envoy of Legate Publius Crispus, here to negotiate the release of his son, Tribune Crispus."

"You have a strange way of conducting negotiations, Roman."

"Would you have responded to more cordial overtures?"

"No."

"I thought not. Now, I have been sanctioned to spare your life and those of your men, if you hand over the tribune peacefully. There is no need for anybody else to die today, Donabedian."

"Tell me first how it is you know my name?"

"I know a lot of things; it is my job. I have spies everywhere, even amongst your own men."

"You lie."

"Do I? Ask yourself this: how did we gain entry to your town so easily? How did we know where to find you hiding?"

"I was not hiding, Roman."

Corvo's men laughed at this and the Armenian leader bristled with indignation.

"Now, what's it going to be, Donabedian? Will you let the tribune go, or do we have to do this the hard way?"

A tall warrior clad in black, with an old scar down his right cheek, said something to Donabedian but his gaze never left the Romans. Donabedian glared at the other man and replied in a harsh tone, though neither Corvo nor Arus understood what had been said.

"Forgive my second-in-command. Dumar is a brave and skilled warrior, but lacks certain social skills and occasionally forgets his place." By the chastened look on Dumar's face it was evident he spoke or at least understood some Latin. "Now tell me, why should I trust you, Roman, when you have just claimed to have turned some of my own men?"

"Oh, you probably shouldn't, but you don't have many other options. You either hand him over and walk away alive, or you die here, now," replied Arus.

"And if I kill your tribune?" asked Donabedian.

"Then I will have come a long way for nothing, and you would still die, but you'd get to reflect on your decision whilst nailed to a cross." Terror registered on Donabedian's face at the thought of being crucified. He threw down his dagger and uttered something in his own language. His men began to drop their own weapons. It took more harsh words and a withering look from Donabedian for Dumar to comply.

Corvo stepped forward. "See to the tribune, Arus. You —" he pointed at Donabedian — "show me where the rest of our men are. Atilus! Guard these men. If there is any trouble from one of them, kill them all."

"It will be my pleasure, Centurion," said Atilus.

"Lucius, bring six men and follow me," said Corvo. He turned to Donabedian. "Take me to our men now."

CHAPTER 16

Corvo could tell that they were nearing the prisoners long before they arrived outside the door to their cell; the stench of stale sweat, urine and faeces had assaulted his nostrils the moment they had entered the corridor.

"Open it," commanded Corvo.

Donabedian slipped a key into the lock and turned it. Then he pushed the door open.

Corvo immediately covered his mouth and nose with his tunic sleeve. Behind him his men did the same. If they had thought the smell in the corridor had been bad, the stench that wafted out of the cell now was unbearable.

"Fetch me a torch," Corvo commanded and within moments one of his men passed one to him. With his mouth and nose still covered, Corvo held the torch aloft as he entered the cell. It was pitch-black and Corvo heard shuffling as the wretches inside scurried back into the furthest recesses, away from the torchlight.

"Soldiers of Rome, I am Centurion Marcus Ovidius Corvo of The Damned, and I am here to set you free." There was no response. "Tribune Crispus is free and Donabedian and his men are our prisoners. I will withdraw with the torch, but please come to the corridor — you are free men once more."

Again nobody moved or spoke. Corvo started to slowly back away towards the door, wondering if perhaps these men were no longer capable of being saved. Just then somebody in the darkness spoke. It was a cracked and small voice, uttered from a throat as dry as the deserts of Numidia.

"Who in Hades are The Damned?"

Corvo peered into the darkness. A pale and gaunt face with sunken eyes slowly emerged.

"It is a long story, my friend," said Corvo, smiling, "but one I will happily share with you when we are away from this place." The man stepped forward. He was nothing but bones and rags, yet the flash of steel in his eyes revealed a determination to survive.

"I am … was Optio Maximus Valens of the Fourth Legion."

"It is good to meet you, Valens. Now, why don't you lead your people out of this filth and into the daylight, where food and water await you?"

Valens nodded and then called a series of names into the darkness. Slowly, a number of shapes began to emerge from the dark cell, squinting in the light. Valens looked about him. "Where is Proximo?"

Another man shook his head. "He is gone, brother."

"I will have my men search this place with torches. If any others still live, we will find them," promised Corvo.

Silence fell as seven men made their way into the large hall. Two could barely stand and were supported by their fellow prisoners. All were painfully malnourished, with long hair, taut cheeks and sunken eyes. But they were still proud men, and refused help from Corvo's soldiers. Instead, they helped one another, a camaraderie forged in the depths of deprivation they had endured together.

Corvo's men stared open-mouthed at their legionary brothers, while Donabedian and his men watched the prisoners in disgust, as if their appearance was somehow their own fault.

An angry muttering started somewhere to the rear of the room and slowly rippled through the gathered men. Corvo watched with alarm as some of his men began to reach for their swords. It was Atilus who drew his weapon first and stepped towards the nearest Armenian.

"Atilus, hold!" roared Corvo.

Atilus glared at Corvo. "Do you not see what these bastards have done to these men? If they were my brothers, I would not hesitate to avenge them."

"I see only too clearly," replied Corvo.

"Then what are you waiting for?" There was more angry muttering, accompanied by the sound of more weapons being drawn.

"Stand down … all of you."

Narek approached Corvo and spoke quietly into his ear. "Centurion, your men are right. These men must die for what they have done."

"It is not your concern, Narek. These men are Romans, not Armenians."

"True, but as your friend I am telling you that if you do not allow vengeance, you risk losing the support of your men."

"My men will do as I say, or pay the price."

Narek held up his palms in supplication and backed away.

Traianus stepped forward. "If you are not going to execute them, then what do you plan to do with them, Centurion? Take them back to Rome to face justice? I tell you now that I for one will not sleep knowing that any one of these animals could escape and slit our throats during the night. You said all enemy soldiers were to be killed."

"I know what I said, but you will do what I tell you to do, Traianus. Sheath your sword."

The man glared at Corvo defiantly.

"I will not tell you again."

"It is I you should be angry with, not the centurion," said Arus. "I promised the Armenians that they could walk away with their lives if they threw down their weapons and took us to the prisoners. So what do you say, are you going to sheathe your sword, or do you wish to make an enemy of me?" The old Roman fixed Traianus with a cold stare and after a few tense moments, Traianus sheathed his sword. Others followed his lead, Atilus the last to comply.

From the corner of his eye, Corvo saw a blur of movement. One of the prisoners had grabbed a gladius from a legionary's belt and thrust it with what little strength he possessed into Donabedian's stomach, before collapsing to the ground from the exertion. The strength of the thrust was not enough to kill the man outright or quickly. The men in the hall cheered and two of them stepped forward to help the prisoner back to his feet. Corvo was surprised to see that it was Valens who had stabbed Donabedian.

Flavius stepped towards the wounded Armenian, who had fallen to his knees, clutching his stomach, and drew his sword ready to put the man out of his misery, but Corvo caught his arm and gently shook his head. Flavius stepped back without a word. The room fell silent as the occupants watched Donabedian lose the fight, finally collapsing in a pool of his own blood. Letting him die slowly had gone some way to appeasing his men, going by the murmur of approval Corvo heard.

"Get these prisoners secured in the cell where our men were kept. Lucius, can you see to the care of our men? I need to find Titus and check if the town is secure." Some of Corvo's men immediately set about leading the Armenians to the cell in a none too friendly manner and Corvo wondered if they would all make it there. Arus was talking with the tribune.

"Tribune, it is good to finally meet you," said Corvo, joining them.

The tribune offered a wan smile. "Apologies, Centurion, you have not caught me at my best."

"I'm sure we can forgive you this once, Gaius," said Arus, smiling.

"By the gods, Cornelius, it is good to see you," said the tribune.

"As it is you."

"How fares my father? He is well, I trust?"

"Our journey here has taken many months, you understand, but the last time I saw him in Rome after our time on the Dacian border, he was in good health. He will be all the better once he knows you are alive and free."

"He thought me dead?"

"No. Never. Had he done so we would not be here, would we? He never gave up on you. He knew you would find a way to survive."

"Many have not," said Gaius, casting his gaze down. "Why have I survived and not the others?"

"I don't know. I suspect that they realised you were an important hostage and could be useful, and so they weren't quite so harsh with you. Those men that have survived with you are the toughest and most robust."

"We lost so many. The things they did … they…"

"It doesn't matter now. Now we need to see to your wounds and feed you all a good meal."

"And I need a bath. Gods, how I miss bathing."

"Yes, I wouldn't disagree that you would all benefit from one, as indeed we all could, but there are no baths here. There are, however, plenty of wells and the sun is warm, so that will have to suffice. Come, let us get you outside so you can feel the warmth of the sun on your face once again."

"Then you'll take me to the wells?"

"Then I'll take you to the wells."

"Good. Because I'm going to drink them dry."

Arus laughed and helped the young tribune to his feet.

"Can you oversee what needs to be done for these men?" asked Corvo. "I need to check that the town is secure."

"Of course," replied Arus.

Nodding his thanks, Corvo started to walk away.

"Centurion Corvo," called the tribune.

Corvo turned.

"Thank you. Thank you all."

Corvo nodded again and then left.

That evening, those soldiers who were not on guard duty gathered in the hall to eat, drink and share stories of the day's battle. Narek and some of his men were also present, the rest out patrolling the streets. A curfew had been imposed on the town by the Romans to try and protect the town's citizens from further bloodshed. Corvo knew that pillaging was often the way of the victorious army, but the actions of Narek's men had horrified even the most callous amongst Corvo's men. However, Traianus had started to grumble that they were being denied their share of the spoils. To try and appease his men, Corvo had told them they were free to plunder whatever they found, the Roman soldier long having supplemented his pay in this way.

"I'm all for a victorious army letting off a bit of steam, but Narek's men are going too far," added Galba to the gathered officers. "Some of our men want to join in and some want to put a stop to it."

"They will do neither," said Arus.

Corvo looked at the old Roman and raised an eyebrow. "And why is that?"

"Because to secure their help I had to agree to Narek having a free hand in the town once it was taken, without interference."

"But..."

"There are no buts, Centurion. We couldn't have taken this town without their assistance. Therefore, we will turn a blind eye to all that goes on, and that's an end to it. That said," Arus continued, "I want to be away from this wretched town as soon as possible. The sooner we're back amongst civilisation, the better. Now, what of the freed hostages?"

"The tribune is asleep," replied Flavius. "He has washed, and even had a haircut and shave. He begins to look Roman again. Two of the other prisoners have died. I am no medicus, but I would say that the first died from the shock of being freed. The second died from overeating. He was warned — they all were — that despite their hunger they should only eat little and often, until their bodies re-acclimatise, but this one didn't listen. Brutus found him wading through our supplies. It is hard to criticise the man when all he has known for months is starvation."

"And the others?" asked Corvo.

"Two more have wounds that they will not recover from and cannot be moved. One has a broken leg which was not reset. The other has a festering wound that has turned black and smells putrid. He will not live much longer."

Corvo and Arus exchanged a look.

"I will do what needs to be done," interjected Galba.

"You're going to kill them?" Flavius asked.

"You said it yourself — they cannot travel, and we must."

"Then why did we bother rescuing them? We may as well have left them festering in that cesspit. If we do this, then we are no better than Narek's men."

"Better they die like soldiers of Rome with swords in their hands than waste away in the dark," said Corvo. "What about the others?"

"The remaining three should recover in time."

"Time is something we do not have," said Arus. "It will not be long before the Armenians or Parthians show up and realise the town has fallen. The sooner we leave, the better."

"Then you will likely have another three corpses on your conscience," snapped Flavius.

"My mission was to rescue the tribune's son. We have achieved that."

"You're a callous —"

"You forget yourself, Optio," interrupted Arus icily. "You'd do well to choose your words carefully the next time you address me."

"It's been a long day, and we are all on edge," said Corvo. "Go and see to the freed men, Lucius."

Flavius stared bitterly at his friend and then stood and strode away.

"You must forgive Lucius, Arus. He holds very high standards for himself and those around him. He is a good officer and a good man for it."

"I know," replied Arus with a sigh. "The matter is already forgotten. You will deal with the other matter?" Corvo glanced at Galba and nodded solemnly. "Good, then I will bid you both goodnight." Corvo watched as Arus strolled over to where Narek was sitting. The Roman accepted a cup of wine and sat down next to the Armenian. They were soon deep in conversation.

"I wonder what that is about?" said Galba.

"No idea. Sometimes, with that man, I think it is better not to know. Now come, we have grisly business to be about."

Galba downed his drink and followed his commanding officer out of the hall and down a corridor to where the freed hostages were being looked after. Flavius turned to face Corvo and Galba as they approached.

"Marcus, I'm sorry for what I said."

"There is nothing to apologise for. The matter is closed. Where are the two men in question?" Corvo asked, and Flavius pointed to a room. "Then you can leave. Titus and I will handle this."

"I can stay if you wish. I understand you only have the men's best interests at heart. It just seemed such a damned waste to have come so far to rescue them, only to end their lives soon after."

"I understand, but if something like that ever happens to me, I just hope that somebody will have the courage to do the same for me. Now go. We will handle this."

Flavius looked at his best friend and his uncle, and then turned and hurried away. Corvo looked at Galba, took a deep breath, and then opened the door.

Despite the excruciating pain he was in, the legionary with the broken leg managed a smile when Corvo and Galba walked in.

"You don't look like the virgins I ordered," the man said.

"Sorry, soldier, the town is devoid of virgins."

The veteran eyed them knowingly. He had been around the legions long enough to know that sometimes sacrifices had to be made. "Well then, I hope to the gods you have come to offer me a soldier's death rather than leaving me to waste away here with nobody for company but this poor wretch who no longer knows where he is."

Corvo and Galba glanced at the young man in the next cot and saw that he had indeed taken leave of his senses. He was muttering incoherently to himself. It was a sad sight.

"Legionary Potitius, isn't it?" asked Corvo.

"It is."

"Tribune Crispus tells me you have served in the legions for nearly twenty years. Is that correct?"

"A little over, actually — man and boy. There aren't too many countries in the Empire I haven't marched through, and there aren't many hairy-backed barbarians I haven't killed. I was with Centurion Galba here in Germania a few years back," he added, looking at Galba.

Galba nodded. "You were in the front line next to me when they counterattacked near the river crossing."

"I was," replied Potitius proudly.

"That was a fine day."

"It was a bloody day," corrected Potitius.

"That it was, but a glorious one too."

"Those days are over for me, Centurion."

"I know, my friend."

"I'm sorry, Potitius," said Corvo. "We are deep in enemy territory and have to travel quickly and lightly if we are to have any chance of evading capture. We cannot take…"

"The badly wounded. It is all right, Centurion, you are doing me a great honour. I have lived a good life and seen much, and I would like to have seen more, but these bastards put paid to that. I want to go out with a sword in my hand, not a bedpan."

"Spoken like a true son of Rome, Potitius," said Corvo, reaching for his gladius.

"If it's all the same to you, sir, I would like you to see to the boy first."

Corvo nodded and turned to face the young man, who stared at him with bewilderment. The smell from his wounds was almost overpowering.

"He was a game lad, Centurion," said Potitius from behind Corvo. "When his wounds turned septic from lack of treatment, he retreated so far inside his own mind that nobody could reach him."

Corvo nodded and turned back to face the young man, but he was too late. Galba had placed one of his big hands across the lad's mouth and very quickly run a knife across his throat.

"Sleep now, boy. Your days of pain are over," said Galba, wiping his knife clean on the bedsheets. He gently closed the young man's eyelids before pulling the sheet over his face.

Corvo stared at Galba but said nothing.

"Best not to tarry or think about these things, Centurion. He isn't the first and I don't suppose he will be the last man that I will have to put out of his misery."

Nodding, Corvo turned and offered his gladius, pommel first, to Potitius. "Die well, Legionary Potitius. The emperor thanks you for your service."

Potitius nodded. "Give me a few moments to make amends with the gods, will you? I have been neglectful of late."

"We'll wait outside," said Corvo.

"Don't drink all the wine in Elysium before I get there," said Galba, clasping the other man's arm.

"I can't make any promises, so best you're not too long in joining me."

Galba grinned. "Farewell, Potitius."

Potitius nodded and watched the two men head for the door. "Centurion," he said suddenly, and Corvo turned to face him. "Get the other lads home."

"I will."

Corvo turned and left the room quietly, shutting the door behind them.

Later that day both men were buried with a full military guard next to their two comrades who had died shortly before them. Corvo had ensured that the men received an extra food and wine ration that evening.

It irked Corvo that in addition to the tribune, they would only be taking three extra men back to Rome to be reunited with their families. How many had originally been taken into captivity? Scores? Hundreds? Only the tribune would know and when the man was sufficiently recovered, he would ask him.

Three days after taking the town, Narek had sent half of his force out just after dawn. When Corvo had asked where they were heading, Narek had been vague and said that they were scouting the area for enemy soldiers in readiness for Corvo's departure. The next day, what remained of Donabedian's men were turned out of the town gates to a chorus of jeers and insults from the town's new garrison. Dumar and his men were given no horses, weapons, food or water. When Corvo had protested that it was a death sentence, Arus had shrugged and walked away.

It was on the seventh day after they had taken the town that they came, a line of black dots on the distant horizon. An eagle-eyed sentry had spotted them and sounded the alarm, and every man who could bear arms had quickly taken up a position on the walls. It was immediately apparent to Corvo that they did not have enough men to properly defend some of the ramparts, let alone the whole town.

"Looks like you were right, Arus. We should have taken our leave the day after taking this place," said Flavius, as the officers and Narek watched the horsemen draw up in line on a sand dune out of arrows' reach.

"No, the centurion was right. If we'd tried to move then we'd have lost more of the freed men, maybe all of them."

"We might still," said Corvo, as he watched the line of horsemen start to descend the dune towards the town. "We won't be able to hold the town for long against that lot."

"Nor will you have to, my friend," said Narek, slapping Corvo on the shoulder.

"And why is that?"

"Because that is my cousin Zoreba with the rest of my men. You can stand your men down now."

"You have more men?" asked Corvo.

"Of course! Did you think that these few men with me were all that opposes Parthia and their puppet king? Please, stand your men down. My cousin will not feel welcome if he is greeted by steel and arrow."

Corvo glanced at Arus, who simply raised an eyebrow in response. Their existence was apparently news to him too.

"Give the order to stand down, Centurion Galba," said Corvo, as Narek descended the steps to the gate to greet his cousin. "But tell them to keep a wary eye," he added more quietly.

"You don't trust them, Centurion?"

"It's the first I've heard of these men joining us here — it makes me wonder what other secrets Narek keeps from us."

Galba nodded before bellowing the order to stand down.

When the riders were just a hundred paces from the town, Galba gave the order for the gates to be opened and the horsemen galloped in to the cheers of Narek's men. Corvo estimated that there were a hundred riders, and as he glanced around, he found he recognised a few faces. Either the men that Narek had sent out to scout a few days earlier had run into the other party, or it had been a prearranged meeting and the story about scouting had been just that — a story.

Corvo and his fellow officers were introduced to Zoreba. The man seemed cordial enough, but his smile never quite reached his eyes, which darted around, taking in his surroundings and searching for weaknesses. It wasn't the behaviour of an ally, and only served to raise Corvo's suspicion.

That evening, those who did not have duties to perform gathered in the large hall for a celebration. The food was surprisingly good and the wine plentiful, but as the evening progressed, Corvo realised that unlike before, the Romans and Armenians were keeping very much to themselves rather than mixing, almost as if a dividing wall had been erected between them. Something had changed, but Corvo was unsure what that was.

"Is it me, or has the atmosphere turned decidedly chillier?" asked Flavius, leaning in close to Corvo.

"I'm of the same opinion. Keep your wits about you and your sword close."

To Corvo's surprise, the evening passed without incident, men from both armies gradually drifting away to their cots once the effects of the wine kicked in. Corvo had been one of the last to leave and although his departure had been acknowledged by Narek, there was no warmth in it. Corvo had expected to struggle to sleep, but had in fact slipped into a deep wine-induced slumber the minute his head touched the pillow. He was woken roughly by somebody shaking his shoulder and found himself staring up into the angry face of Narek. Corvo was alert in an instant and quickly swung his legs over the edge of the cot. Behind Narek were two well-built Armenians, their swords drawn.

"What is the meaning of this, Narek? You betray us?"

"It is not us who do the betraying, Roman, but your army. It is time for you to leave."

"Leave? What are you talking about?"

"Zoreba brought grave news. Your legions have moved out of their border forts and have put the people of Crixia to the sword: men, women and children."

"I know nothing of this. Besides, is that not what you and your men did to this very town less than a week ago?"

"This town was held by traitors who deserved to die. Crixia was a town loyal to me. You Romans have killed your allies and cannot be trusted."

"Something must have changed. The commander of the Romans must have received intelligence that the town was held by forces loyal to Parthia and her sympathisers. Rome does not betray her allies."

"It appears that she does now. Enough talk. Get to your feet, Roman."

"You're making a huge mistake, Narek."

"No, it is you Romans and your arrogance who have made the mistake."

"We can't leave — the tribune and the others are not yet recovered enough to travel."

"You think I care, when Romans have put hundreds of women and children to the blade? Zoreba thinks we should execute you all, but I have fought with you and bled with you and so honour dictates that I spare your lives. But I advise you to travel swiftly and avoid running into me or my men, as I will not show such clemency again. Now on your feet."

Corvo had no choice but to comply. He stood and went to leave, but Narek called him back.

"Centurion, your sword." Narek held the weapon out for Corvo, who snatched it from his hand. "Please do not make me regret my decision." He brushed past Corvo, down the corridor and out into the bright sunshine. Corvo followed, flanked by Narek's two guards.

Outside, Corvo's men were standing in the town square, including the freed prisoners and the walking wounded. Corvo knew that at least two of his men had grievous wounds from the battle a few days earlier and had been bedbound.

"Where are my seriously wounded men, Narek?"

"Alas, they will not be accompanying you. Their end was swift and honourable."

"You had no right to do that."

"Do not seek to lecture me, Roman, not when your countrymen have committed such butchery in Crixia. Consider yourselves lucky — I have spared your lives, let you keep your weapons, and even given you precious water and food. It is more than you deserve, but my sense of honour is satiated. That is an end to it."

Corvo glanced around and saw that his men were indeed carrying their weapons, but they were outnumbered and weren't wearing armour, and would be unlikely to prevail. As an extra safeguard, Narek had posted archers on the ramparts with arrows nocked. At the first sign of trouble, Corvo's men would die before they'd even had the chance to draw their swords.

"Time to go, Roman," said Narek.

Corvo strode forward. "Give the order to march, Centurion Galba."

Galba nodded and then bellowed for the men to slow march out as the gates were pulled open for them. Corvo watched the last of his men leave and then turned and glared at Narek.

"There is one thing you should know, Narek."

"And what is that?"

"Rome never forgets. Rome never forgives." Corvo turned and strode through the gates after his men. Behind him the gates slammed shut, not only on the town, but also on their alliance.

CHAPTER 17

The men had been walking for nearly two days. The hot sand of the plain was finally behind them and the valley with its high sides and shady outcrops brought some much-needed relief from the baking sun. One of the scouts had come running back to report to Corvo, but by then Corvo and everyone else had already seen the carrion birds circling high above them. Having suffered a long march with little water, the panting scout was unable to immediately make his report. Corvo handed him his waterskin and the man gratefully took two huge swills before making his report.

"Bodies ahead, sir, about twenty of them," the man finally managed to relay.

"Romans?"

"No, sir, Armenians."

The way the man fidgeted told Corvo he had something else to impart.

"What is it, Legionary?"

"They've been … tortured, sir, dismembered. Others have been nailed to trees…"

"Show me," said Corvo. "Centurion Galba, have the men rest here, but stay alert. There's still a chance that Narek will change his mind and follow us. Post sentries in every direction. I shouldn't be long."

Galba nodded and marched off to pass on the instructions. Corvo fancied he heard a collective sigh as the men fell out to rest and take a drink or relieve themselves.

"Lead on, Legionary."

The scout led Corvo and Flavius further into the valley and over a small rise, where the second of the two scouts Corvo had sent ahead of the column waited patiently.

The sight that greeted them was one of horror. Bodies were strewn around the small clearing. Some had been nailed to trees and appeared to have been disembowelled. Others had been staked on the ground and left to burn in the fierce sun. Some had lost ears or hands, others arms and legs. When the men who had done this to them had moved on, the carrion birds had moved in and feasted on their eyes.

Corvo had seen many brutal things during his time in the legions, but this was barbarity for the sake of it, and whoever was responsible clearly enjoyed inflicting pain and suffering.

"Who were they, do you think?" asked Flavius.

Corvo didn't immediately answer as he strode over to one of the corpses. The man had been staked in the sand and carved up with knives. His head had been cut off and placed on his torso, but still there was no mistaking his identity. It was Dumar, Donabedian's second-in-command. Corvo looked around and saw that all the bodies were wearing a black uniform; these were the men Arus had spared in return for the tribune's life. They had sent them out into the desert with no horses, weapons or water and this had been their fate.

"They are the men we exiled from the fort, Donabedian's men. This is … was Dumar."

"Who did this to them?"

"If you recall, Narek sent out a large number of men the day before we turned these men out. They were supposedly out scouting, but they brought back no fresh intelligence."

"You think Narek sent his men out to lie in ambush for these men?"

Corvo nodded. "If you recall, Arus was deep in conversation with Narek. I think Arus asked Narek to send his men ahead to lie in wait for them. This butchery is of their making."

"Then why not just have the Armenians killed when we took the town? Once the tribune was free, he could have had them executed. It would have found favour with our men, as you know. Traianus would have been more than willing."

"He promised them that they could leave the town unharmed. He gave no such guarantees once they had left the town," said Corvo.

"But why the butchery?"

"I think Narek's soldiers were settling a feud with men they perceived as traitors."

"What do you want to do?"

"We'll camp for the night, where the men have stopped. It's not worth pushing on now."

"And what about these men?" asked Flavius, indicating the bodies.

"Let them stay as they are. They are not our men." Corvo strode off back down the valley.

"Is this what you had in mind when you ordered Narek's men to set an ambush for them?" asked Corvo the next morning as he and Arus at the site of the slaughter.

Arus glanced at the grisly scene as the rest of the column passed through. "I asked them to kill these men, as they were a loose end. I could not do it in the town as I had given my word. The fact that they have been overzealous in their duties is hardly down to me."

"You call this overzealous? I call it butchery. To think I fought alongside the animals who did this."

"What does it matter, Corvo? Dead is dead. We couldn't have taken the town and rescued the tribune without the Armenians' help. So they've gone too far. It doesn't matter. These men were enemies of the Empire."

"So too are Narek and his men. Do you know anything about this massacre he claims took place at Crixia?"

"No, nothing. How could I? I've been here all the time."

"True, but men like you have ears everywhere."

"Yes, we do, and you should be grateful for that. Besides, whoever did carry out the attack…"

"Massacre," corrected Corvo.

"…at Crixia must have had his reasons. It is not for us to judge. Now come, or we will fall behind the column. We have rescued the tribune and three other men, we are alive, and we're heading towards the Syrian border. This is cause to be happy."

"I shall be happy when we cross the border and don't have to keep looking over our shoulder wondering if Narek has changed his mind and is racing up behind us to butcher us like these men."

Corvo shook his head and took one last look behind him. He thought he could see movement on the far horizon, but in the haze of the sun he couldn't be certain. He turned and hurried back to the column, which, despite only being able to move at the pace of its slowest member, was still making good speed.

To the west of Vermuk lay the Roman province of Syria, and it was from the forts based along its border with Armenia that the Roman legions now marched. Whilst Corvo and his men might have been unable to outrun any pursuers, by travelling west they hoped to run into a Roman column travelling in the opposite direction, which would at least give them some protection. Unless they themselves attacked. Corvo and his men were still dressed in local attire and from a distance would be easy to mistake for Armenians. This had been foremost in his mind as he pushed them harder every day.

"Some of the men are struggling, Marcus," said Flavius as he walked beside his friend on the fourth day since leaving Vermuk. "Especially the former hostages."

"You think I don't know this, Lucius? If I don't push them, we're all going to be caught by the Armenians following us."

That was news to Flavius. "We're being followed by Narek and his men?"

"No, I don't think so. There looks to be too many of them to be Narek's men."

"Then who?"

"Does it matter?"

"They could be our side," said Flavius hopefully.

"If they are, it's likely they've been defeated and are themselves being pursued. Why else would they be travelling back towards Syria? No, I suspect it's an army of Armenians loyal to King Tiridates, or Parthians, probably searching for the Romans that sacked Crixia."

Flavius cast a nervous look behind him. "Can we outrun them?"

"The border is still seven days' march away and I believe they are no more than a day behind us." He left the question unanswered.

"Well, we can't stand and fight."

"I'm aware of that, Lucius," snapped Corvo. "I've spoken to Titus, and he confirms that there is a fort about a day's march west from here which should have a garrison."

"And how long is it since Titus was last here?"

"Some time," conceded Corvo.

"Then let us pray that it is still there and intact."

Late the following afternoon they arrived on a small rise overlooking a plain. No more than a mile away, still intact and inhabited judging by the small plumes of smoke that curled lazily into the sky, was the Roman fort of Lipa. What Corvo and his men couldn't tell was whether it was occupied by Romans or Armenians.

"What do you think?" asked Arus as the small cluster of officers stared over the plain at what they hoped would be sanctuary. "Our boys or theirs?"

"Ours. The Armenians would probably have destroyed it once they took it," replied Corvo.

"But they haven't destroyed it in all the years it's stood here. Why would they do so now?"

"So as not to provide shelter for any invading force. They might have been using it to garrison their own troops until recently and we've displaced them."

"It's a gamble," stated Arus. "There is no cover out there, so if you're wrong and they're Armenians, or worse still Parthians, we'll be cut to bits by arrows or ridden down by their cavalry."

"If you have a better idea, then now is the time to give it voice … any of you," said Corvo, looking at his fellow officers.

"Look — riders," said Flavius, pointing. Two horses had appeared from the far side of the fort, heading for the main gate.

"Can anybody make out their uniforms?" asked Corvo. He was greeted by silence.

"Legionary Faustus!" shouted Galba, looking over his shoulder. "Get over here."

Faustus hurried over and snapped to attention. "Sirs."

"Faustus, your eyes are sharper than ours. Those riders approaching the fortress gates, are they Roman or Parthian?"

Faustus shaded his eyes with his hand and stared hard. "Ours, sir," replied the young soldier confidently.

"Are you sure?" asked Flavius.

"Positive. So too are the men on the ramparts."

"You can see men on the ramparts?" asked Galba incredulously.

"Yes, sir."

"Damn, I'm getting old."

"Thank you, Faustus, you may go," said Corvo, smiling.

Relieved that he wasn't in any sort of trouble, Faustus nodded and walked away. Several of his comrades approached him immediately, wanting to know why the officers had called him over.

"Well, that's a relief," said Flavius.

"True, but I'm not sure it's the solution to our problem," said Arus.

"What do you mean?" asked Flavius.

"He means that it's only a small garrison fort; we're not going to find a couple of legions camped there. Our odds against the following army have improved only negligibly." Earlier that day, Corvo had decided to share with the other officers that a large force of enemy soldiers was hot on their heels. None had seemed surprised and Corvo had found himself wondering how many others had seen the dust cloud for themselves.

"I seem to recall speaking to you before about working on your motivational speeches, Marcus," said Flavius, grinning. Slowly, the others started to smile and then they burst into laughter, drawing inquisitive looks from the nearby men.

"Well, it's better than nothing, I suppose," said Galba. "At least we'll have a roof over our heads and some grub. Do you want me to prepare the men to move out?"

Corvo looked at the darkening sky and shook his head. "By the time we cross the plain it will be dark, and I don't want some fresh-faced legionary panicking and putting an arrow into one of us. We'll camp here for the night and move at first light."

"What if the Armenians march through the night? They'll be upon us by morning," said Flavius.

"I don't think it likely; they haven't done so far. Nevertheless, pick good men to keep watch tonight; they are to wake me if they think our pursuers are moving." Flavius nodded. "I think the men will all be glad of a rest. Tell them to get as much sleep as they can, as we will be moving out at first light. There are to be no campfires tonight."

Later that night, Corvo stood atop the ridge staring eastwards towards where the enemy had stopped for the night, their camp easy to find by the myriad pinpricks of light from torches and campfires.

"By the gods, there must be thousands of them," said Flavius, handing Corvo a drink, which he gratefully accepted. "That fort and the men in it aren't going to be anywhere near enough."

"They are all we've got."

"We could keep marching and try to outrun them."

"You said yourself that some of the men are struggling to keep up the pace, so I don't think we'd get very far. Besides, whether we stay or run, they are going to fall on that fort. It wouldn't feel right to run and let those men in the fort die just to buy us a day or two at most."

"You're right, I know. But to have come so close just to die here at the hands of an enemy force that weren't even looking for us, seems cruel."

"Well, they're looking for us now. Their scouts came close to the rear of our column today; they know we're here and where we're going."

"Then our lives are in the hands of the gods," said Flavius ruefully.

"And the hands of our brothers. Go and get some sleep, Lucius. I shall need you strong and alert tomorrow."

Flavius downed the last of his wine and smiled at his friend. "Goodnight, Marcus."

"Goodnight, Lucius."

Corvo had tried to get a few hours' sleep himself, but had awoken every hour or so. Sometimes it was the snoring of a soldier nearby; sometimes he imagined he could hear Armenian soldiers invading the camp, killing his men in their sleep. Sometimes it was the biting cold. By the time the sun started to peek over the eastern horizon, Corvo was up and preparing to move out, a bundle of nervous energy despite the lack of sleep.

Corvo gave the order to form up so that he could address the men.

"We have reached the fortress of Lipa, with a small Roman garrison. As you are all no doubt aware, we have a large force of enemy soldiers on our tail. They were not pursuing us and were in all likelihood heading for this fort, and then the Syrian border. We just happened to have the misfortune to run across their path and now they have our scent too. We can't outrun them, and we can't in good conscience leave the men in that fort to face them alone."

"Why not?" asked Traianus. "Our mission was to rescue the tribune and then get home to a pardon and freedom. None of us signed up to die in some fortress in the middle of nowhere." A number of men murmured their agreement.

"None of us did, but we can't outrun them anyway. Leaving now would buy us a day or two at most, and then they'd come after us and we'd be caught out in the open. I don't need to tell you how deadly the Parthian mounted archers are — we'd all be killed without ever getting close enough to smell their breath. I for one would rather face them from behind the walls of a fort with a garrison at my back." More murmuring, this time in support, mostly from the professional soldiers in the ranks, but also from the gladiators, who would always prefer to look their enemy in the eye than be killed by an arrow in the back.

Corvo was about to say something further, but one of the sentries he had posted was frantically gesturing. Corvo looked at the man and immediately understood what the man was signalling.

The enemy was coming.

CHAPTER 18

Their arrival had been spotted the moment they had descended the slope and started to cross the plain. Although Corvo could not make out what was being shouted, it was clear that orders were being barked and men were rushing to obey.

The fort gates opened, and two riders came galloping out. They had obviously seen that the newcomers had no cavalry with them, and they could therefore risk sending a small reconnaissance party out. Corvo noted that both men were wise enough to stay outside of bow range.

Aware that they were dressed like Armenians, Corvo had been careful to march the men like Roman legionaries, in one column, four men wide, and displaying their shields. As the riders drew near, the men kept steadily marching towards the fort without missing a step or taking any aggressive stance. The riders observed this small force for a minute or two, and then turned and raced back towards the fort, no doubt to report back. It would be easy for the fort commander to assume that they were Armenians and had simply taken the shields and swords from dead Romans. Corvo just had to hope that the commander was discerning enough to realise that if they were planning on attacking the fort, they would need a lot more men than Corvo had with him.

The gates were firmly shut once both riders were safely within the fort's sanctum.

Corvo brought his column to a halt just out of bow range of the ramparts, shouting the order unnecessarily loudly so that the fort's inhabitants would recognise the Latin dialect. After removing his Armenian helmet to show his short dark hair,

Corvo told Galba to hold the men where they were while he went to talk with whoever was in command of the garrison. A restraining hand prevented him.

"I think I stand a better chance of being recognised as a Roman citizen than you, Centurion," said Arus, smiling. "You don't get too many grey-haired and balding old men in the Armenian army, I dare say."

Corvo couldn't disagree, but the risk of losing Arus to an arrow wasn't one he was prepared to take, and he told him so.

"Nevertheless, Centurion, I will go. And that's an order. Just be sure to flay the man who does fire the arrow," said Arus.

Arus lowered his hood and slowly stepped forward, his arms splayed out in a gesture of supplication. He had got to within a hundred paces of the gates before the first arrow punched into the sand not two strides in front of him. Arus looked at the arrow with disdain before casting his gaze at the dais above the fortress gates.

"That's far enough," called a portly centurion, identifiable by his traverse helmet plume. "Who are you and what do you want? Speak quickly before we use you for target practice."

"My name is Cornelius Arus, a staff officer from Legate Publius Crispus' camp. The men behind me include a tribune and three of his comrades who we rescued from Vermuk. They require medical attention and rest, so I would be grateful if you would open the gates and let us in."

"I have my orders, and those orders are not to open the gates to anyone but legionaries."

"If you look closely, you will see that they are legionaries. Now, I suggest that you open these gates and let us in, or you'll find yourself reduced in rank and serving on the northernmost reaches of the Empire on permanent latrine cleaning duties."

Arus was about to say something further when Centurion Galba strode past him towards the gates. He had also removed his helmet. Another arrow landed in front of Galba, but he pointedly walked a few paces past it before stopping. There was a murmuring from the ramparts as the centurion leant forward to peer at the large man below him.

"Titus! Titus Galba, is that you?" called the centurion. "It's me, Portius."

"I know. Nobody else would be so stupid."

"What are you doing with these Armenians?"

Galba sighed. "They are not Armenians, Portius. None of us are. We are Romans, and the man behind me is who he says he is and more."

"Apologies, sir," said Portius, turning his gaze towards Arus. "I take my duties very seriously and have never seen you before."

"Then you should count yourself lucky," replied Arus bitterly. "People who vex me in the way you just have don't normally get a second chance."

"Portius?" called Galba, exasperated. "The gates?"

"Yes, of course." Portius turned to the men guarding the gates. "Well, what are you waiting for? Don't keep the officer waiting — get those bloody gates open!" he bellowed.

The heavy plank holding the gates shut was lifted by four legionaries, and then two others pulled the gates open before stepping back out of the way.

"Finally," muttered Arus as he gestured for the column to follow him in. "Thank you, Centurion Galba," he added as he strode past the big man.

Once inside the fortress, Corvo gave orders for the former hostages and his wounded to be taken to the medicus, and for the rest of his men to be found accommodation and fed.

Finally, after satisfying himself that enough sentries had been posted, including Legionary Faustus, whose eyesight was superior to most, he asked Portius to lead the officers to a briefing room. An orderly brought them bread, fruit and watered-down wine and closed the door behind him. Corvo turned to the men seated around the table. Arus, Galba, Flavius, Nerva, Tribune Crispus, Portius and an optio from the fort's garrison whom Corvo did not know looked at him expectantly.

"Do you command here, Centurion Portius?" asked Corvo.

"I do now, sir. Optio Lentelus here is my second-in-command. We had a young tribune, but he marched out with two thirds of the men nearly two weeks ago and we haven't seen or heard from them since."

"I think we might know what has happened to them," said Corvo.

"Sir?"

"First, how many men are garrisoned here?" asked Corvo.

"Now? About a hundred and twenty," replied Portius.

"About? You don't know?"

"I haven't had a chance to carry out a roll call for some time," said Portius, reddening.

"How many of these are combat-ready?"

"One hundred and nine, sir," interjected Lentelus. "There are others in the medical bay who should be capable of manning the walls. Two are seriously ill, but the rest are a collection of sprains, broken bones and malingerers. I was going to discharge some of them onto light duties this morning anyway."

"Thank you, Lentelus."

Portius glared at his second-in-command, but the other man held his gaze. Corvo didn't think there was any love lost there.

"Well, men, a little under a day's march from here, approaching from the east, is a large force of enemy soldiers. They are marching on the border forts, I suspect, but your little fort stands in their way, so they can't leave it standing. I also suspect that your missing tribune and his men have run afoul of them."

"Are they Armenians or Parthians?" asked Portius.

"I don't know, and it doesn't matter — they will all bleed and they will all die on Roman swords."

"You can't be serious, sir?" said Portius. "You plan to stand and fight them?"

"Yes. My men and your troops will have to hold off a force many times its superior."

"We'll be slaughtered," protested Portius.

"You will if you desert your post, because if they catch you out in the open, they will show you no mercy. We've seen what they do to prisoners, and it isn't pretty. But it's nothing compared to what I will do if any of your men try to slip over the walls at night."

"And just how long do you expect to be able to hold out here?" asked Portius bitterly.

"For as long as it takes for a relief force to reach us, or until the last arrow has been expended and the last sword broken. We are making our stand here like true Roman soldiers. Right, Lentelus, please take Centurion Galba on a tour of the town's defences and armoury. I want to know how many javelins we've got, how many archers, where we're strongest and where we're weakest. Lucius, please get some of the men working on collecting rocks — anything light enough to hurl but heavy enough to maim or kill — and have them positioned in piles around the ramparts. Portius, you and I will visit the hospital and see who is capable of fighting, or at the very least able to throw rocks at the enemy. Nobody but the dead and dying will be permitted to sit this out. Sextus, you're in charge of lookout. Have men positioned on every wall, with your best men looking east."

"How long do we have until they get here, do you think, Centurion?" asked Lentelus.

"I would imagine we'll see their advance units first thing tomorrow morning, with the rest showing up around noon. That is why we cannot afford to waste a single moment. Any more questions? No? Good, then see to your tasks."

"Where do you want me?" asked Arus.

"You, Tribune Crispus and the three other hostages will take the best horses and make a break for it to the west, towards the border. I can only spare you a couple of men as protection, but hopefully you won't need any. We've endured too much to let the tribune get killed or captured defending this place. Besides, if he doesn't get back, these men will not be granted their freedom, and by the gods they deserve it."

The tribune shook his head. "Out of the question. You and your men have risked your lives to save us. I will not turn my back on you now when you need us."

"I appreciate the sentiment, Tribune, but a half dozen swords aren't going to sway this battle one way or the other. Let our deaths, if that is what Fate decrees, not be in vain. If we can enter Elysium knowing we rescued you and your comrades and also bled the enemy on these walls, then we can hold our heads up high."

"We're staying and that's an end to it," snapped the tribune.

"With respect, Tribune, you may outrank me, but I command here, and I am commanding you to leave."

"Technically, I command here, Centurion," said Arus. "You were in command of the mission to rescue the tribune, which you've done."

"Semantics, Arus, and you know it. They are not rescued until the tribune is back in Rome, or at least Roman territory, which, incidentally, lies just a few days' ride that way," said Corvo, pointing west.

"Perhaps, but there is no guarantee that we will make it, so perhaps it is better that we remain here — safety in numbers."

"Look —" began Corvo.

"I need to redeem myself," said the tribune suddenly. Everyone around the table stared at the young man. "I let myself down, I let my men down and, worst of all, I let my father down when we were taken prisoner. I cannot face him with that stain on our family's reputation. I need to win back some honour."

"All you are likely to find here, Tribune, is death," said Corvo softly. "We are outnumbered and have little hope of relief."

"Then it will be a glorious death, and my father will think better of me for it."

Corvo knew it would be hypocritical of him to deny the tribune the one thing he himself was constantly striving for. Honour.

"Very well, you may stay, Tribune. There is, however, no need for you to remain, Arus. You should leave and take the other three men with you."

Arus looked at the tribune, who nodded his agreement.

"Go, Arus. Tell my father that I chose to stand with brave Romans and died with honour. Losing his son *and* his best friend will be too much for him to bear."

"That's kind of you, young Gaius, but I'm an old man who's tired of running. I think I'll stay."

"When did you last kill a man, Arus?" asked Flavius.

"At Vermuk. Don't worry about me, Optio Flavius. You don't get to be my age with a lifetime of service to the Empire without being able to look after yourself."

Corvo raised an eyebrow. "Very well, stay. What of your men, Tribune?"

Gaius smiled. "They too have a score to settle."

"So be it. We stay together, we fight together and by the gods' good graces, we live or die together. Courage and honour."

"Courage and honour," the men replied in unison.

"One thing," said the tribune, as the men all got to their feet to see to their duties. "I don't even know what legion you men are attached to. I should like to know with whom I fight."

"We are the Legion of The Damned," replied Corvo, smiling.

"Fitting."

"You have no idea, Tribune," said Corvo, laughing as he left the room. The others followed. They had a long, hard day ahead of them.

It was late in the afternoon and the shadows were growing long when the shout went up from a sentry on the eastern wall. Nerva had immediately sounded the alarm and soon, Galba, Flavius and Lentelus were bawling at the men to assume their positions on the ramparts. Corvo had organised the men into sections, with men allocated either rampart duty or resupply duty. Those on the ramparts would be the first to face the enemy attack and would consist of two ranks which would rotate throughout the battle. They would be supported by any man capable of using a bow, and although some of Portius' men claimed to be proficient archers, their numbers were still too low to make a real difference.

Behind the ramparts and in the square below, Corvo had assigned men to two strategic reserves. These soldiers would be used to reinforce any part of the ramparts that looked like they might fall, and also to protect the gates should they look like they would be breached. Galba and Flavius would each command one of these reserves. Atilus had been earmarked as one of the commanders, but when he heard that he was once again to be held back, the gladiator had railed against the centurion. Corvo had merely smiled and clasped the other man's arm. He told him he would be honoured to fight alongside him. Corvo, against the wishes of Galba and Flavius, had placed himself in the front rank of the eastern rampart force and Atilus would be to his right.

Corvo assumed his position and glanced about. He was pleased to see that his now enlarged force had followed orders quickly and efficiently, with all walls manned and the two strategic reserves of twenty-five men each formed up smartly below. He turned his attention to the distant horizon, but could see no sign of the enemy.

"Who called the alert?" shouted Corvo.

"I did, Centurion," replied a young soldier from the garrison force who looked to be only a few years younger than himself.

"Why did you call the alert? I can't see anything," said Corvo, keeping his voice even.

"I thought I heard something, sir, and then I saw a rider, there, in the distance." The young soldier pointed. "I thought it best to call a stand-to."

Corvo looked back out over the ramparts towards the ridge from where he and his men had emerged only yesterday. Half a dozen dark spots had appeared on the ridgeline.

"Stand-to! Stand-to!" Corvo bellowed. Word spread along the ramparts like wildfire. "You did well, Legionary. What is your name?"

"Servius, sir. Thank you, sir." The young man beamed and then turned to resume his position on the ramparts.

Corvo was suddenly aware that Portius had sidled up alongside him.

"What are you doing here, Portius? You were told to position yourself with Second Section."

"Yes, I know, but as commander of this fort I thought you'd want me near you for advice once the alarm was sounded."

"What I want, Portius, is for every man to follow my instructions and do what he's told, whether he be the cook or a centurion. We are so short-handed that if just one man leaves his assigned position, it could lead to a problem. Do you understand?"

"Well, yes, but —"

"No buts, Portius. Now go."

Portius sloped off to resume his position, muttering under his breath.

"They got here quicker than we thought," said Arus, joining Corvo.

"It's just their scouts. My guess is that the cavalry isn't far behind, but the bulk of their force won't arrive until mid-morning tomorrow," replied Corvo.

"Should we chase them off?"

"What with? We have a few horses but no professional cavalry. They'd either disappear before our men reached them or they'd knock them out of their saddles with arrows before they even got close. Besides, I could be wrong, and their cavalry might be hiding out of sight, just over that ridge."

"I preferred your first assessment. One more night of peace would be nice."

"You'll get it. They won't attack tonight, maybe not even tomorrow. Depends on how hard their commander has been pushing them." As he spoke, Corvo watched the horsemen turn their mounts and disappear down the far side of the ridge. He knew that the next time they appeared they would have company, a lot of it.

CHAPTER 19

Despite his belief that the Armenians wouldn't launch a night attack, Corvo ensured that the sentries were rotated every two hours. He didn't want to risk anyone falling asleep on watch.

The total fighting force under his command was eventually determined as one hundred and seventy-two, with just three men bedbound. To look after them and the stream of wounded that would soon begin falling once battle was joined, there was what passed as a medicus and Brutus the cook. Brutus had made it clear to Corvo that he would rather be on the ramparts with a gladius in his hand. Corvo, however, had insisted, telling him that at some point, it would probably be necessary for him to do just that.

Just after first light, Corvo had completed a roll call and was relieved to find that nobody had tried to run, not even Portius. They had all heard about the riders appearing on the distant ridgeline and Corvo had no doubt that loose tongues among his own men had already told the fort's garrison what was heading their way. If any were shocked or frightened, they didn't show it. Instead, they stood stoically, listening as Corvo outlined his plans to defend the fort. The men had already been allocated their assigned positions for the coming battle, but until now they hadn't been aware of quite how large the force ranged against them was. In truth, Corvo didn't know either. They had only seen the enemy force from a distance. It was enough to know that they outnumbered the Romans by a considerable margin and that there was nowhere to run. They stood and fought, or they died with a spear or arrow in their back. They were Romans, he reminded them, and Romans didn't shy from a fight. They would turn their fort into a fortress of steel and the enemy army would break upon its walls like a wave on a cliff.

"That was definitely one of your better speeches," said Flavius, as they watched the men disperse. "You're undoubtedly getting the hang of it."

Corvo laughed. "Well, we've done all we can. Now our fate is in the hands of the gods."

"And the courage of the men manning these walls."

"Let us hope that is enough."

"Come, let's go and see what delights Brutus has found in the garrison stores. I don't know when we will next get a chance to eat." Flavius slapped his friend on the shoulder and together they made their way to the mess hall.

The riders appeared on the ridgeline several times that morning. Sometimes just a couple of riders, sometimes as many as twenty. It wasn't clear whether their intention was just to keep an eye on the fort and its inhabitants, or whether it was to unsettle and tire out the defenders whom they knew would have to run and man the ramparts every time they appeared. Either way, tension permeated the air and nerves were starting to fray.

"Why don't they just attack?" snapped Flavius.

"Because their full force isn't here yet," replied Corvo.

"Then why keep sending horsemen to the ridge?"

"To keep us on edge."

"Well, it's working. I for one will be glad when they just attack."

"We'll make a gladiator of you yet."

Both men turned to see Atilus had joined them.

"Atilus, is all well?"

"It is. I just fancied a different view."

"How do your men fare?"

"They feel the same way as Flavius; they just want it to begin."

"It won't be long before they get their wish," said Corvo as he watched the horsemen depart again, leaving the ridgeline empty. He suspected that the other side would be a different sight altogether.

Corvo spent much of the day walking the ramparts, offering an encouraging word to his men and checking that everything was as he had ordered. Piles of stones and rocks had been gathered at various points along the ramparts, simple but lethal weapons to drop on an attacker's head. Almost every javelin the garrison possessed had been placed along the ramparts, ready to be hurled once the attackers came into range of the deadly missiles. Whilst Corvo knew that the main attack would focus on the gate and the eastern wall, he still had to allocate men, javelins and rocks to the other three walls. The enemy would no doubt probe these for weaknesses.

The day dragged on, the lack of activity even starting to grate on Corvo's nerves. The enemy had not shown their faces again during the day and had it not been for the orange glow of a myriad of campfires which lit the distant night sky, Corvo could have believed that they were alone out there.

Corvo's dreams that night were haunted by a black-clad horseman racing towards him as he stood alone outside the fort gates. Instead of riding him down, the horseman simply galloped past him, Corvo's sword strokes doing nothing but passing through the rider heading into the fort. He woke with a start. Breathing deeply, he rose and went outside. He decided to walk the ramparts and check on the sentries.

He was standing on the eastern rampart gazing towards the distant ridgeline as the sun slowly woke from its slumber and started to climb into the azure sky. It was going to be a gloriously hot day. For many, it would be their last. Corvo heard the tramp of hobnailed caligae as the sentries were relieved and fresh soldiers took their place. Corvo nodded at them as they assumed their position and encouraged those being replaced to go and get some rest. The men were subdued but had a steely determination about them. Corvo watched them go and with a last glance at the lightening sky to the east, he followed them down the steps to find something to eat.

The first riders showed up around mid-morning. The alarm was raised and Corvo slipped on his helmet and rushed up the steps to the eastern rampart. Being back in a Roman uniform gave him pride and confidence, and he hoped his men felt the same way. The fort's quartermaster had blanched when Corvo told him he was acquisitioning all his uniforms and armour, but had relented once Arus assured him that he would not be in any trouble. Corvo had insisted that if they were going to die, they were going to die dressed as soldiers of Rome.

All around, the men of the garrison took up their assigned positions, those who had just been woken from their slumber hastily trying to fit their armour and strap on their swords as they ran.

Corvo stared out over the plain towards the ridgeline where the riders had gathered and formed a long black line.

"How many?" asked Arus.

"Two hundred, perhaps more."

"Are they about to attack?"

"I think they will probe our defences prior to attacking." As the words left Corvo's mouth, the riders urged their horses forward.

They came slowly at first, picking up speed as they drew near to the fort's walls. As they reached bow range, they fanned out in both directions and began firing arrows at the men on the ramparts either side of the gate.

"Shields!" bellowed Nerva, not waiting for Corvo to give the order, and immediately the men on the ramparts knelt down and raised their shields to protect themselves. Most of the arrows sank into the wooden palisade or shields, whilst others cleared the ramparts and thudded into the sand in front of where Flavius and Galba stood with their strategic reserves. Neither man flinched nor raised their shield.

To his right, Corvo heard a shout of anguish. A legionary Corvo didn't recognise had an arrow through his right forearm.

Another volley of arrows thudded against the defences and Corvo shouted for the men to keep their heads down and their shields up. A few moments later Corvo heard the sound of horses galloping away. He cautiously got to his feet and, lowering his shield just enough to peek over, saw that the Armenian horsemen were withdrawing. What he saw behind them made the breath catch in his throat.

"Stand-to!" he bellowed. "Come on, on your feet." Advancing over the ridgeline was a dense mass of infantry. They weren't formed up into organised blocks like the Roman cohorts marching in step with shining armour and helmets, but instead advanced in crooked lines. They were no less intimidating.

And they kept coming.

Line after line crept over the ridge until there were almost too many lines to count. Corvo estimated there might be as many as five thousand men gathered on the plain, and he didn't know if that was their full force or whether thousands more patiently waited out of sight for their chance to join the fray.

Galba and Flavius had left their positions at the head of the strategic reserves to join Corvo.

"There must be thousands of them," said Flavius.

"About five thousand, I estimate," replied Corvo. "They might be concealing more."

"Now there's an encouraging thought."

"Just means there's plenty to go round," said Galba, smiling. "Make sure you leave some for us, Centurion."

"I don't think that will be an issue, Titus," said Corvo, drawing strength from the older man's calm demeanour. "Courage and honour."

"Courage and honour," echoed Galba and Flavius, and the three men clasped arms.

"I'll see you both afterwards," said Corvo.

"You will. As I recall, it's your round," grinned Galba.

"To your positions, men."

They nodded at Corvo and descended the steps to resume their station with the reserves. Corvo glanced around. Some of the men, especially the younger ones like Servius, were looking at him, though whether they were awaiting orders or seeking encouragement, he didn't know. He turned to face the fort and raised his voice.

"Shortly, the enemy will try and take this fort. There are many of them and we are few. But they are barbarians, and you are Romans. They are no match for you." The men cheered. "We have this fort, we have the men of the garrison, and we have The Damned." Another cheer, louder this time. "We will not yield, we will not retreat, and we will not die!" The cheering reached a new level. "Let them try and take this fortress of steel, for we are in the mood for blood!"

The cheering escalated until Corvo's men started chanting "The Damned," whilst the garrison men started to chant their cohort's number.

Satisfied he had done all he could to instil some courage into his men, Corvo glanced below and saw Flavius give him a thumbs-up and a wide grin. Then he turned to face the plain. The Armenians were still formed up in lines, but a passage divided them into two blocks. Corvo knew that this was to allow the cavalry through. They would race ahead and provide covering fire as the ranks of light infantry approached the fort. He could try and take some of them out with the few archers he possessed or with their precious supply of javelins, or he could wait and order his men to shelter beneath their shields until the storm abated, but by then the infantry would almost be upon them. It was a difficult and potentially deadly choice.

The Armenian cavalry had started to advance. Corvo made a quick decision. He would wait out the storm of arrows and save their projectiles for the massed ranks of the infantry.

"Mounted archers approaching. Prepare shields!" shouted Corvo. The order was given just in time and almost as one, the troops on the ramparts and those forming the reserve crouched beneath their shields. Whilst the front two ranks of Galba and Flavius' men stacked their shields on top of one another, building a wall, the rear ranks lifted their shields above their heads, overlapping one another and constructing an almost impregnable testudo. A hail of arrows battered their shields while others peppered the ramparts, most either burying themselves in the wooden palisade or the roof of one of the fort's buildings.

Corvo glanced to his right and caught Servius' eye. The young legionary looked petrified and Corvo gave him a reassuring smile. Gradually the sound of the arrows started to die down and Corvo thought that he could hear the enemy's horses retreating. Offering a silent prayer to the gods whilst at the same time gesturing for Servius to remain beneath his shield, Corvo slowly rose to his feet.

No arrows came at him and, as he had suspected, the Armenian mounted archers were indeed retiring. The massed ranks of their infantry, however, had used the cover of the arrows to race towards the fort.

"On your feet!" bellowed Corvo, and his men instantly responded. "Archers, fire at will." Immediately, those who claimed to be proficient with the bow began to fire into the advancing tide of men. "Javelins!" shouted Corvo. He knew he had to time this right. The javelins had an effective throwing range of about thirty-five strides, though from their elevated position they would travel further. When the front rank was about fifty strides from the fort's walls, Corvo gave the order to throw.

He watched as the javelins arced into the sky and then plummeted down towards the enemy. He had timed it perfectly, and he watched with satisfaction as countless Armenians were knocked off their feet by the iron barbs.

Still they came on in their hundreds.

There was just time for one more volley, Corvo decided.

"Javelins!" Within moments his men were ready to unleash the second volley. This time they would be throwing downwards, and at much closer range. With the attackers so closely packed together, it would be almost impossible for his men to miss, and from that range they would be killing throws. "Release!" Corvo had no time to assess the casualties as some of the enemy were already preparing to scale the walls with ladders. "Swords!" On his command, half the men along the eastern rampart drew their short swords and made ready, whilst the remaining men proceeded to drop or throw rocks at the enemy below.

The bravest of the Armenians were starting to climb. By chance, the first man to reach the top of his ladder appeared in front of Corvo, and he was immediately rewarded with a powerful gladius thrust to the head. It was all Corvo could do to pull his weapon back out before the man's body fell backwards, taking two warriors on the same ladder with him, their screams lost in the noise of battle.

Corvo had a few precious moments before more men climbed the ladder and he risked a glance around. A large Armenian clad in black had reached the rampart and was driving Servius back towards the edge. Out of nowhere, Atilus appeared and parried the Armenian's next thrust before pushing him back over the parapet with his foot. Atilus immediately rushed over and, shouting for Servius to help him, grabbed hold of the top of the ladder which was loaded with Armenian soldiers. Together they tipped the ladder backwards, sending the men tumbling to the ground below.

Corvo turned back to his own ladder just as another Armenian reached the top and thrust his sword at him, slicing along his left forearm. Corvo recovered quickly and brought his gladius down in a chopping motion, severing the Armenian's outstretched arm below the elbow. Wide-eyed, the man stared at the bright red blood that spurted from the stump before Corvo slammed the iron boss of his shield into his face, sending him plunging back to the ground below.

Along the eastern wall the soldiers were desperately trying to stop the attackers from breasting the parapet, but as soon as they tipped one ladder over, another went up in its place.

The Armenians waiting at the base of the fort's walls were subjected to an almost constant barrage of rocks and stones hurled by the men stationed above. They were losing men by the score, yet still they kept coming.

A roar from his right drew Corvo's attention and he watched as Servius charged with his shield at a man climbing over the parapet. Servius slammed into the man, sending him back, yet somehow, the Armenian managed to cling on to the ladder. Servius was on him in a moment and thrust his gladius into the top of the man's chest. When Servius pulled it free, the Armenian slowly fell back, taking the man behind with him.

A clang against Corvo's shield alerted him to the fact that someone was again at the top of his ladder, and he adjusted his stance ready to drive the man backwards. But this warrior was powerful, and he landed blow after powerful blow against Corvo's shield. Corvo soon found himself being driven back.

Someone shouted a warning and Corvo glanced round to see three Armenians making their way along the ramparts towards him. The sword of the Armenian on the ladder thundered into his shield again, sending a painful jolt down Corvo's arm.

Corvo risked a look over the rim of his shield and saw that his opponent was now over the parapet and grinning at him. He was extremely tall for an Armenian and powerfully built. He gestured for Corvo to attack him and Corvo obliged. Leading with his shield, he sliced low at the man's thigh, but the Armenian had anticipated Corvo's move and stepped back just in time before launching his own attack. There was no finesse in his assault; his plan was simply to use his superior strength to batter Corvo until he could no longer raise his shield.

Corvo braced against the forceful downward cuts and could feel his strength leaving him. Gambling all, he waited for the Armenian to pull his sword back ready to launch another blow and then quickly slammed his shield down onto the man's foot. The Armenian howled with pain but didn't go down, so Corvo thrust forward with his gladius. Again the man had anticipated Corvo's attack and managed to twist away, and instead of receiving a fatal stomach wound, he suffered a gash to his left side which did nothing but infuriate him. He slammed his sword down into Corvo's shield twice more, the second stroke having the desired effect as Corvo slipped on blood and fell backwards, his shield dropping from his grasp. Sensing victory, the big Armenian stepped forward and, grasping his sword with both hands, prepared to drive the blade deep into Corvo's chest. Just as he was about to deliver the killing blow, his body jerked. He slowly turned to look behind him, and it was only then that Corvo could see the two arrows embedded between his shoulder blades. Above the gate behind the Armenian, Corvo caught sight of one of the Syrian brothers, but couldn't tell which one. Corvo quickly leant forward from his fallen position and swept his gladius in a powerful horizontal arc which struck the Armenian's leg at the ankle, severing his foot. Roaring with pain, the Armenian toppled backwards. Corvo wasted no time. He scrambled to his feet and drove his blade into the man's throat.

Corvo turned and watched as Atilus, like the god of the arena he had once been, killed the last of the three men who had been approaching Corvo along the ramparts. A cheer broke out from the men below who had been watching and soon spread when somebody shouted, "They're retreating."

Corvo stood and looked around. There were still a few Armenians on the ramparts, men who had been engaged in a fight when the order to retreat was issued and who now couldn't extricate themselves, but the men on the ladders and those below were indeed retreating. Realising that their own men had gone, those Armenians left stranded by their comrades threw down their weapons. They were either run through or pushed backwards over the parapets. The Romans expected no mercy. They in turn would offer none.

When the last Armenian had been despatched, the men all started to cheer and wave their weapons in the air.

"Thank you, Atilus," said Corvo, as the other man strolled over to him.

"You're welcome. Though if they'd managed to get more men over the wall, we'd be having this conversation in Tartarus now."

Corvo looked about him. The rampart and the ground beneath the wall was thick with enemy dead. There were also many dead Romans. There would be far fewer men manning the walls the next time the Armenians came. And come they would.

"We must have killed nearly three hundred of them," said Servius from nearby.

Corvo thought it probably nearer two hundred, though the enemy wounded would be nearly as many.

"Then we only have another four thousand seven hundred to kill before we can rest," said Atilus breezily. "Keep your wits about you in future, boy. I may not be there to save you next time."

Looking abashed, Servius fixed his gaze on the plain, where the Armenians were regrouping at the foot of the ridgeline.

"Keep a sharp lookout, Atilus. I need to speak to my officers."

"Take your time. It's not like I am going anywhere," grinned Atilus.

Corvo descended the steps and gestured for Galba, Flavius and Nerva to attend him. "Sextus, I need to know how many javelins and arrows we have left. And how many rocks. Titus, we took a battering up there. I want you to take two out of every three men on the other walls and send them to the eastern rampart."

"That will leave those walls dangerously undermanned. They'd never hold in another attack."

"I know, but we should see any attack coming from a long way out, and we can reinforce the walls as necessary."

"Why not just use our men to replace our losses on the eastern wall?" asked Flavius.

"Your men will be needed, and soon, I think. If it hadn't been for Atilus' quick reactions, we would have been overrun already. Don't wait on my command — if you see a breach, then move in to deal with it. Flavius, I want you to get me a casualty count." His three officers nodded and left to carry out their allotted tasks.

A short while later, Corvo was sitting in the shade and trying not to dwell on how close he had come to being killed. Galba was the first to report that the men from the other walls had been redeployed. Nerva then reported that there were hardly any rocks left, no more than three arrows remaining to each of his archers even after collecting the enemy arrows lying around, and that only one javelin remained per man. When the enemy came next time, they were not going to be able to thin their numbers anywhere near as well as they had done during the first assault.

"Then let's retrieve those weapons outside," said Flavius. "I know the shanks sometimes bend on impact to prevent the enemy from being able to use them, but they will be better than nothing and some will be serviceable."

The same thought had crossed Corvo's mind. He stood and strode up the steps to the eastern rampart, his officers following close behind.

"Nothing has changed," said Atilus, as they approached.

"We were just considering trying to retrieve some of our javelins and arrows," said Corvo. "We don't have enough to hold the enemy back otherwise."

"Then let's do it."

"Their mounted archers will be on us in no time. If we open the gates, we may not be able to close them again. I don't think it's a good idea, Centurion," said Galba.

"You're probably right, Titus. It's not a risk we can take. We'll have to make do with what we've got."

"What we've got isn't enough, Marcus," said Flavius.

"Well, it will have to be. If we hold them outside the fort, we have a chance. If they manage to get in, we're finished. My decision is made. We stay in the fort. Now haul up all the ladders we can reach. Let's not make it easy for them."

The enemy didn't attack again that day, and Corvo assumed they were either licking their wounds or trying to devise a new plan to take the fort. That they would eventually take the fort was not in doubt, and the only way for his command to survive was to make the Armenians pay such a high price in blood, that they would decide it was no longer worth trying. It was a forlorn hope, but it was the only one Corvo had.

After checking that the sentries were set for the night and then calling in to the makeshift hospital to check on the wounded, Corvo found himself a quiet corner to settle down for a few hours' sleep. He had told Nerva, who was officer of the watch, to wake him at the first sign of movement by the enemy. It seemed that his eyes had only been closed for the briefest time before someone was shaking him awake again. Corvo was surprised to find that it was in fact the middle of the night.

"Centurion… Centurion!" The voice was insistent.

"Yes, what is it?" answered Corvo grumpily. He opened his eyes to see a nervous-looking Faustus staring down at him.

"Optio Nerva told me to fetch you, sir. He asks that you join him on the eastern rampart."

"Are we under attack?" asked Corvo, leaping to his feet.

"Not that I'm aware of, sir."

"Then what is it?" demanded Corvo.

"It's best the optio tells you, sir."

Corvo bit back a retort — the lad was only carrying out his orders and may not know what the issue was. "Lead on, Faustus."

Faustus turned and hurried towards the steps leading up to the eastern rampart, Corvo hot on his heels as he fastened his belt and sword.

"What is it, Sextus?" asked Corvo without preamble.

"Atilus and some of his men, sir, they've gone over the wall."

"What?" Corvo instinctively leant over the parapet to see if he could spot them, but the plain before him was pitch dark. "How many?"

"I don't know, sir. Atilus and his men took over the watch from me and my lads, but when I came out for a piss later on, I couldn't see anyone up here except him." Nerva pointed to a former gladiator by the name of Sertorius, who was lying unconscious on the rampart floor.

"And what happened to him?"

"Legionary Felix did, sir." Nerva pointed to one of the men who they had liberated from the quarry, a man who stood at well over six foot and had fists the size of cabbages. "He didn't take well to Atilus and his boys running out on us like that."

"But why desert now? It makes no sense," said Corvo, as he examined the three ropes hanging from the parapet down to the ground below.

Behind them, Sertorius was finally coming round.

"What happened?" he mumbled, glancing around. His eyes alighted on Felix. "You… I'm going to…" His words died on his lips when he saw Corvo leaning over him.

"You've got one chance to speak the truth, Sertorius, so I suggest you take it. My patience is all but exhausted. Why has Atilus deserted?"

"Deserted? He hasn't deserted."

"Then why have he and some of his men stolen away over the walls in the dead of night?"

"Because I asked them to," said a familiar voice behind Corvo.

Corvo spun round to find Arus standing behind him. "You told my men to desert?"

"Of course not, Centurion. They haven't deserted. They've gone on a foraging mission."

"What?" said Corvo, incredulous.

"I sent them out to retrieve javelins."

Corvo stared at Arus, but before he could say anything, one of the ropes started to shake violently. Corvo dashed to peer over the side, expecting to see a number of Armenians scaling the rope, but instead he saw Atilus. He looked surprised to see Corvo.

"Pull them up. Pull them up," he hissed.

"Felix, pull them up," ordered Arus, and the big man immediately made light of hauling the rope up. When it reached the parapet, Corvo could see that at the end of the rope was tied a bundle of javelins and he immediately rushed over and helped lift them over the parapet. The other two ropes were also shaking now and Felix, Arus, Nerva, Faustus, Corvo and Sertorius worked to bring the bundles safely into the fort. By the time they had hauled the gladiators up and over the walls, they had lifted nine bundles of javelins and a quantity of arrows. Corvo estimated there were over one hundred javelins lying on the rampart.

"Optio Nerva, get these javelins distributed along this rampart," ordered Corvo. To the east the sky was just starting to lighten, while below him the fort was beginning to stir, and the next shift of sentries was slowly making its way towards the steps. "And tell these men to be alert."

"Yes, sir."

"Arus, Atilus, a word," said Corvo. He stormed down the steps towards one of the buildings. "Out!" he bellowed to two men sitting in a small room near to the makeshift hospital ward. He waited for the men to leave before slamming shut the door. "What in Hades did you think you were doing?" This was directed at Atilus. "You could have got yourselves killed and for what — a handful of javelins? You could have denied me some of my best men. And you —" he turned to face Arus — "I am in command of this mission. You do not go giving orders to my men behind my back."

"Calm down, Centurion. All is well. Atilus was only following my orders and yes, you are in command of this mission … up to a point."

"Up to a point?"

"Yes, and that point was reached yesterday. I believed you made an error in not trying to retrieve weapons from outside the gates, so I approached Atilus to see if his men were prepared to do it, and they were."

"You cannot undermine me like that. I'm either in command or I'm not. Which is it?"

"You are."

Corvo closed his eyes and took a deep breath, acutely aware that the medicus, Brutus, and everyone in the hospital ward next door would have heard their argument. It wouldn't do to have the men think that the officers were at odds with one another.

"Very well. It is done. We will speak of it no more. Thank you for your efforts, Atilus, and those of your men. It was a brave thing you did."

Atilus nodded. "How much difference it will actually make, I don't know."

"Well, it should count for at least a hundred more Armenian dead, but more importantly, it is a small victory for us and will boost morale. It will also make the enemy wonder if we have a huge arsenal of javelins —" His words were cut off by a loud knock on their door.

Atilus strode over and pulled it open. Filling the doorframe was the impressive figure of Felix. "Sorry for the intrusion, sirs, but the enemy are here." The man said it so matter-of-factly that it took a moment for the news to register, but when it did, the three men squeezed past Felix and out into the square. Galba was already ordering the stand-to and all around them, men were rushing to their positions.

Corvo headed up the steps to the eastern rampart and stared out at the plain.

The enemy had indeed come. And this time, they had brought everyone.

CHAPTER 20

Corvo watched as a mass of men and horses manoeuvred across the plain. The infantry had split into four groups, with the largest in the middle and three smaller ones on its flanks and to the rear. The cavalry, predominantly mounted archers, had lined up in front once again.

"I think they mean business this time," said Nerva.

"I didn't think they were fooling around yesterday," replied Corvo, allowing himself a small smile.

"Well, it just means we'll all have to work that bit harder to earn our pay."

"Let's just hope we're around to spend it afterwards."

"What do you think they'll try this time, sir? An all-out frontal assault, throwing everything at us?"

Corvo studied the Armenians as they finalised their formations. "No, that didn't go so well for them last time." His eyes suddenly widened as he realised what the Armenians were planning. "They're going to hit us on three sides at once this time. The two smaller forces will hit the north and south walls and the larger force will be thrown against the gate and this wall."

"And the fourth formation?" asked Nerva.

"A reserve held back to exploit any openings." Corvo turned to shout down to Galba and Flavius, who were standing ready with their strategic reserves. "Lucius, Titus. They're going to attack the south and north as well as the east. Send half of your men to reinforce each wall. Titus, you go and take charge of the north wall. Flavius, you take command of the reserve. Wherever it's needed, you go. Don't wait for orders." He turned back to Nerva. "Sextus, you go and command the south wall, but tell Atilus he has command of the troops above the gate."

Nerva saluted. "Courage and honour."

"Courage and honour," Corvo responded as Nerva turned and hurried away, shouting at Atilus to take command of the gate and its guards as he passed by.

"Here they come!" someone on the gate shouted. With a great roar, the horde started to march towards the fort, their cavalry leading the way and acting as a screen.

After a while, the archers began to gallop towards the fort before reining in, just out of javelin range but well within bow range. Behind them, the Armenian infantry were deployed as Corvo had anticipated, the majority marching towards the eastern wall whilst the two smaller forces peeled left and right to assault the south and north walls.

"Shields!" bellowed Corvo, and once again his men crouched down behind their shields to protect themselves from the rain of arrows. The bombardment was more intense this time and rather than taking aimed shots, the Armenians sent as many arrows towards the ramparts as they could in an attempt to keep the Romans' heads down so that their infantry could reach the walls unmolested.

Corvo waited as long as he dared and then got to his feet, roaring for his men to do the same. An arrow glanced off his cheek-guard and was harmlessly deflected, but it startled Corvo. The enemy were now at the foot of the walls.

"Javelins." Along the eastern wall and above the gate, his men drew back their javelins in readiness. "Release!" A volley of javelins plunged down into the massed ranks of unprotected flesh below. The screams of men filled the air. "Javelins," repeated Corvo. "Release!" Another volley of iron lanced down onto the Armenians, causing a new wave of agonised screams, but still they came. Most of Corvo's men were now out of javelins, the rest having been distributed to the other walls, although here and there the odd javelin stood unused. "Let them have whatever else you've got," Corvo ordered. His men began to hurl everything that wasn't tied down over the walls, hoping to crush a skull or break bones, whilst the archers fired arrow after arrow, certain in the knowledge that they would hit something.

The Roman archers were noticed by someone in charge of the Armenian archers and, on his command, a score of arrows flew towards the top of the gate where Corvo had stationed his bowmen. Corvo glanced up to see two of his men, including one of the Syrian brothers, fall from the rampart, both hit by multiple arrows. The remaining archers began to fire at the men below, who were trying to batter the gates open. They were rapidly running out of arrows, and would soon be reduced to using any enemy arrows they found lying around.

The first ladders clattered against the wooden palisade and Corvo drew his gladius. "Swords!" he shouted. All along the line his men drew their own weapons and readied their shields. "Send these bastards back to Hades, The Damned." The men roared their war cry, but it was as short-lived as it was loud, as already the first snarling faces were at the top of the ladders.

Corvo slammed his shield into the face of the man at the top of the nearest ladder, sending him sprawling to the ground below. His shield was immediately hit by two arrows meant for his chest.

Another man appeared and Corvo tried to repeat his battering action, but the man was alert to the danger and twisted out of the way. The Armenian thrust his sword forward, nicking Corvo's leg above his metal greaves. Stepping forward, Corvo sliced down with his gladius, but the Armenian's sword was quickly up to block the stroke. In doing so, however, he exposed his chest and Corvo swiftly kicked the man backwards, off the ladder.

Corvo grabbed the top of the ladder to push it over, but was immediately targeted by two Armenian archers. The first arrow thudded into the palisade while the second glanced harmlessly off Corvo's shoulder armour. Corvo instinctively backed away, and that was all it took for first one and then a second Armenian to scramble up the ladder and over onto the ramparts.

Without hesitating, Corvo launched himself at the two men. Using his shield to block the downward stroke of one man, Corvo thrust his gladius at the other, but he turned away just in time and was able to deflect Corvo's thrust. Corvo immediately sliced at the man's unprotected calf, inflicting a deep gash that brought the man to his knees. His comrade launched into a ferocious barrage of blows, all of which were blocked by Corvo's shield. When he felt the man tiring, Corvo put his shoulder behind his shield and rammed into him, simultaneously thrusting his gladius into the man's groin. The howl of pain was unlike anything Corvo had heard before. Turning quickly, he saw that the man with the sliced calf had struggled to his feet and was preparing to attack Corvo. After parrying the Armenian's first two strokes, Corvo brought his blade down into the soft spot where neck met shoulder. He pulled his blade free and then kicked the man backwards.

More Armenians had now cleared the ladder and Corvo watched as one of his soldiers held off three men with a javelin. The Armenians had fanned out around him, just out of reach of the javelin, waiting for an opening. One of them suddenly ventured too close and as quick as a flash, the legionary thrust the javelin tip into the man's chest.

A roar to Corvo's left drew his attention and he turned in time to parry a downward blow from an Armenian, before slicing the man across the stomach. The Armenian crumpled to the rampart as his guts spilled out in front of him.

The legionary with the javelin had downed a second attacker, but was struggling to retrieve his javelin, its barb having caught on the man's ribs. The third Armenian seized his chance and rushed the legionary, but the Armenian's swing merely cut through thin air as the legionary ducked and circled behind him. Pulling a dagger from his belt, he sliced the Armenian across his heel. As the man crashed to the ground, the legionary leapt on him and began to stab him with a frenzy of blows.

As the blood-soaked legionary got to his feet, Corvo saw it was Quintus Faustus, whom Atilus and others had called a coward for not having bloodied his sword in the battle at Vermuk. They had, it seemed, been quite wrong. Faustus looked round for his next fight, and his eyes met those of Corvo. He grinned at the centurion, but his grin turned into a grimace as an arrow struck him in the back of the thigh. Before Corvo could warn him, a large Armenian scrambled over the parapet and thrust his spear through the young man's chest. Faustus locked eyes with Corvo again as blood seeped from the corners of his mouth and he fell to the ground.

Corvo roared with anger and charged. The Armenian reached for his sword but before his hand had even grasped the pommel, Corvo had run him through, shoving his body aside before glancing around to assess the situation.

In the square below, Galba's men were holding the north wall and although hard-pressed, Nerva appeared to have prevented the enemy from gaining a foothold on the south wall. The gates still held and Atilus and his men were trying to support both sides of the eastern wall, but despite their efforts, Corvo could see that it was only a matter of time until they were overrun. Even as he considered this, he watched as a cluster of Armenians climbed onto the far end of the eastern rampart and dispatched the few remaining soldiers there. They had their foothold and Corvo knew that once they had sufficient numbers, they would attack from the flank. It was time to commit the reserve. Corvo signalled Flavius.

Flavius nodded once and then, raising his voice to be heard above the sounds of battle, shouted, "On me — now is your time for glory!" He jogged his men across the square until they were about ten paces from the Armenians, who were gathering numbers above them, before giving the command to stop.

"First Section, javelins." The men of First Section automatically hefted their javelins. "Release!"

The javelins were thrown hard and true, and the tightly clustered group of Armenians all collapsed to the ground, some pierced by more than one javelin.

"Up the steps to the rampart," ordered Flavius. "Second Section, prepare to release javelins. Make them count."

The men of First Section raced up the steps behind Flavius, none of them encumbered by javelins, whilst their comrades followed at a slower pace. By the time Flavius and his men reached the rampart, the next wave of Armenians was climbing over the palisade, but they were too slow and all were met by the bite of cold steel. Once the rampart was clear, Second Section formed up and were preparing to throw their javelins at the men below, when Atilus shouted Corvo's name. Corvo and Flavius both looked up and saw Atilus pointing at the north wall. Galba and a handful of men were outnumbered and being driven back.

"Second Section, javelins at the men on the north wall!" bellowed Flavius. The men turned at his command and made ready to launch. "Titus, get down!"

Titus immediately dropped to the ground, roaring at his men to do the same. Moments later, a salvo of javelins struck the Armenians. Galba was on his feet immediately and ordered his men to charge. At the same time, Flavius ordered Second Section to run to their aid. Together, the soldiers were able to drive the Armenians back over the wall from the ramparts.

Corvo watched in despair as Nerva's men on the south wall began to lose ground, knowing that his reserves had been used up, as had their supply of javelins.

Without needing to be told, the few remaining archers under his command had automatically turned their support to the southern wall, but Corvo could see that it would not be enough. The north wall had been consolidated and the eastern wall had been saved for now, thanks to Flavius' intervention and the sheer savagery with which Atilus and his men fought. But they were going to lose the south wall and with it, the whole fort, as the Armenians would then be able to assail the defenders from every direction.

Then, as Corvo watched, from out of the hospital ward came a stream of men led by Arus, amongst them Tribune Crispus and the cook, Brutus. Some had bandaged limbs, others facial wounds, but none were prepared to shirk their duty. They streamed up the steps and came up behind the Armenians on the south wall. Seeing their wounded comrades coming to their aid, Nerva's men rallied and, on his command, they charged the Armenians. It wasn't the sort of fighting Roman legionaries enjoyed or normally excelled at, their strength lying in their ability to fight in close formations, but today it didn't matter. Today was a day for killing by any means necessary, and Nerva and his men did just that.

It was going to be a glorious end to his first and last command, Corvo realised.

He thrust his sword into the stomach of another Armenian who came howling towards him, and then stooped low to avoid the swing of another man, before despatching him by thrusting his blade into his groin. Corvo stood and awaited his next opponent, but nobody attacked. He glanced round and saw that the number of skirmishes were dying off and the hail of arrows had finally ceased.

A roar went up from the north wall and Corvo turned to see what remained of Galba's men and Second Section cheering and waving their swords in the air. The wall was theirs. Hope flared in his chest as Corvo saw that the last two Armenians on the south wall were also being put to the sword. These soldiers now added their voices to the roar of victory, Arus the most vocal of them all.

The sound of battle had dissipated and all Corvo could now hear was the sound of men cheering. The enemy had been driven back and as Corvo looked out over the palisade, he saw hundreds of men running and limping away, back to the distant ridgeline. The ground below the fort walls was carpeted with bodies. The wounded lay there, crying out in their own language, or attempting to crawl back towards their own lines.

Every now and then a Roman bowman put them out of their misery.

"We've done it. We've driven them off," said Atilus, beaming from ear to ear. He was covered in blood, but none of it his, apparently.

"We've won a small victory, bought ourselves a few hours or maybe another night, but that's all," replied Corvo. He was suddenly bone-tired.

"For the love of the gods, will you not let the men savour this moment? We have just won a great battle and yes, it may well be our last, but these men have fought with honour. Let them enjoy their victory before pissing on their joy."

Corvo's shoulders slumped. The burden of command weighed heavily. "Of course. Our victory is in no small part thanks to you and your men." He placed a hand on the gladiator's shoulder.

"Everyone did their share." Atilus' words reminded Corvo of Faustus and he hurried over to where the young man lay. "He died well, Centurion. I saw him fall."

"As did I. He was no coward."

"No, he was not."

"What are your orders, Marcus?" asked Flavius, joining the men.

"Have everyone take a drink and then get a headcount."

"And a weapons count?"

Corvo shook his head. "It doesn't matter what we have — we no longer have the men to use them."

Flavius nodded and turned to leave.

"Lucius," Corvo called after him. "Thank you. Your intervention saved both walls."

"Wasn't about to let you lot have all the fun, was I?"

Corvo smiled and Flavius resumed his duties.

The headcount, when it came back, was worse than Corvo had anticipated. Sixty-four men were left on their feet with another twenty-seven injured, most of whom were expected to live. The medicus had died charging the south rampart, as had the cook Brutus. The only medical help the wounded would receive now would be what their comrades could provide.

"Well fought, Centurion," said Arus, approaching Corvo.

"Arus. You live!"

"I do."

"That was a brave thing you did — gathering the men from the hospital to support the south wall. You made all the difference."

"But at what cost?" said Arus, eyeing the bodies of Brutus and the medicus.

"Their lives were not sacrificed in vain. You took the wall."

"We did," said Arus, though both men knew they wouldn't be able to hold it for long. When the next attack came, it would all be over.

To their surprise, the Armenians didn't launch any more attacks that morning, nor during the afternoon, and Corvo began to fear that they might be preparing a night assault after all. He therefore had half the men stand watch whilst the other half rested. By the time dawn came, nerves were frayed and tempers were short, but there had still been no sightings of the enemy. Shortly before noon, a line of cavalry appeared on the distant ridgeline.

"They're back!" shouted a lookout. The remaining men able to bear arms wearily mounted the steps to the ramparts. The bodies had now been cleared away, the Romans having been carried down into the square, the Armenians tossed over the side to lie heaped on top of hundreds of their comrades.

Corvo watched the horsemen form up on the ridgeline and sighed. It looked like they had all seen their last sunrise. He had nowhere near enough men to withstand another attack. He just hoped that his father and grandfather, heroes of Rome both, had watched the battle with pride. He wanted to be able to look them in the eye when he arrived in Elysium.

Then something unexpected happened. The horsemen turned and slowly disappeared over the ridgeline. Another shout went up from a lookout. One of the two sentries Corvo had posted to the western wall was waving his arms frantically.

"Men, Centurion, thousands of them!" he shouted.

Corvo and his officers all hurried along the ramparts to where the two sentries were standing. One pointed to the distant horizon, though there was no need, for even Galba and Arus could see the advancing columns.

"The bastards have used the time to march to our rear," said a despairing Flavius.

"But why? One more frontal attack and we'd have been overrun anyway," said Atilus.

"Does it matter? They're going to roll over us whichever direction they come from," snapped Flavius.

Corvo began to laugh.

"Marcus?" queried Flavius. "Marcus … what's so funny?"

"Those men, they're marching in columns."

Flavius cast a glance their way. "Yes, what of it?"

Galba started to laugh. "Armenians don't march in columns — those are our men."

Everyone stared hard at the approaching army, but even those with the poorest eyesight could now see the sun glinting off the polished eagle standards and armour of the legionaries marching four abreast towards them.

"They're our men," said Corvo, echoing Galba.

The legions were coming.

Less than an hour later the combined force of two legions and a large number of auxiliaries came to a stop outside the western wall of the fort. A squad of auxiliary cavalry were then sent ahead to the front of the fort. By now, Corvo had ordered his men to open the gates for the horsemen.

"Who commands here?" asked one of the cavalrymen.

"I do," replied Corvo. "Centurion Marcus Ovidius Corvo of The Damned."

"The Damned?" The cavalry officer looked around at the piles of bodies and nodded. "It is a good name — it looks like you've been to Hades and back. I will report back to the legate." The horsemen turned their horses and departed. It was not long before they returned, accompanied by a number of staff officers. The senior tribune spoke first.

"I hear you call yourself The Damned. What legion are you attached to, Centurion?" he said, addressing Corvo.

"None, sir," replied Corvo. "We are what you might call a scratch force."

"Where are your senior officers?"

"I am in charge of the men, sir."

"I think you are deserters."

"We are, sir, some of us at least."

The senior tribune's eyes widened in surprise and anger. "Marko, return to the column and bring back the guard. These men have just admitted to being deserters and are to be arrested," he said, turning to the leader of the auxiliary cavalry.

"At once, sir," replied Marko.

"Belay that order."

"Who said that?" demanded the senior tribune.

"I did," said Arus, stepping forward.

"Who are you? I'll have you crucified for insubordination." The senior tribune turned to the cavalryman. "Fetch the legate and guard now." The horseman galloped off. "You'll pay for your insubordination with your life — you all will."

A short while later, a rider galloped in whilst the tramp of a hundred pairs of feet could be heard following in his wake as the guard doubled into the fort square and formed up. Corvo's men reached for their weapons.

"What goes on here?" demanded the legate. He looked vaguely familiar, though Corvo couldn't immediately place him.

"These men have admitted to being deserters and this man —" the senior tribune pointed at Arus — "has displayed gross insubordination. I demand that they be punished."

"Cornelius? Cornelius Arus? Is that you under all that blood?" asked the legate.

"Greetings, Tullius. You are a welcome sight," replied Arus. "Where did you spring from?"

"We've been gathering our forces just inside Syria, ready to invade. I am one prong of the invasion force; another has headed east via Crixia." Arus and Corvo exchanged a glance. At least Tullius hadn't been responsible for the massacre at Crixia. "By the gods, we thought you all dead. Publius' son?"

"Gaius is alive. Some decent food, a bath and plenty of rest will see him restored to good health."

"Who is this man, Legate?" interjected the senior tribune.

"This is Cornelius Arus … from Legate Crispus' staff." By the look on the senior tribune's face, it was clear he had heard Arus' name before. "Do you still wish me to instigate proceedings against him, or shall we just say that you may have misheard?"

There was a lengthy pause before the senior tribune replied, "Yes, I was clearly mistaken. I apologise, Legate, Arus." The man's face had turned a deep crimson.

"Centurion Corvo?" said the legate, staring at Corvo's blood-covered face.

"Yes, sir."

"You probably don't recall, but I was in the tent with Arus and Legate Crispus when you were asked to take on this mission."

Corvo nodded as he recalled that fateful night and where he had seen the man before.

"I am impressed that you succeeded, and it looks like you've had a little fun here, too." The legate looked around. "I hope you've saved some for us?"

"There's plenty to go round, Tullius. They went in that direction," said Arus, pointing. "If you hurry, you might catch up with them today."

"We were going to camp here tonight, but I think by then some of these bodies might be a bit ripe in this damned heat, so perhaps we will push on. What happened to the fort's garrison?"

"Some are here with us, but most apparently went out some time ago. We think they probably ran into the men who attacked us and were slaughtered," replied Arus.

The legate nodded. "What will you do now?"

"Return to Rome and deliver the tribune to his father."

"Rome? Of course, you won't know. I'd forgotten how long you've been gone. Much has changed."

"Such as?" asked Arus, looking worried.

"The emperor grows more suspicious by the day and sees enemies where there are none. Legate Crispus is one example. His successes on the battlefield have led the emperor to fear him and as a consequence, Crispus has been sent to the border with Germania to put down a revolt that few believe even exists. It is expected that he will not return, if you get my meaning?"

"But what of my men's freedom and pardons?" asked Corvo. "They have done everything that was asked of them and more. This is not their fault."

"I know, and I sympathise."

"Can you not grant their freedom? Pardon the men? You are of the same rank."

"I am, but no. The papers have all been drawn up, but they are with the legate. There is nothing I can do."

"Then it has all been for nothing?" said Arus. "I can't accept that. I won't accept that."

"But what can we do?" asked Corvo dismally.

"There is only one thing we can do," said Arus. "Go to Germania."

"If you do, I cannot guarantee that the man you find will be the same man who sent you on your mission all that time ago. The loss of his son, the emperor's mistrust and now this posting has all taken its toll. He'd given up on you."

"Then we must not delay," said Arus.

"I wish you luck, old friend." The legate and Arus clasped arms.

"You too. This war will not be easy to win."

"You've made a start," said the legate, looking around at the bodies again. "We will try and finish it." The legate turned his horse and led the men out of the gates.

"So what now?" asked Flavius.

Corvo took a deep breath. "Now I address the men and tell them the truth. Then I leave for Germania with those who would follow me."

He took a last look at the thousands of Romans and auxiliaries marching east and then turned away.

His destiny, it seemed, was in the opposite direction and the forests of Germania.

A NOTE TO THE READER

Dear Reader,

Thank you for taking the time to read *Fortress of Steel*, the first book in the *Legion of The Damned* series. I hope you enjoyed it and will join Centurion Corvo and his comrades when they march on to their next adventure, *Forests of Death*, where they swap the heat of the desert for the snowy forests of Germania.

I have always been fascinated by ancient history, Roman in particular, and have long wanted to write a series of books based on this period. Covering more than a thousand years of history, there is a wealth of tumultuous events and wars to write about. Several famous Roman historians including Tacitus, Suetonius, Cassius Dio and, of course, Julius Caesar, have left some valuable accounts of these events, albeit biased (the victor always gets to write the history), yet there are still enough gaps for a fiction writer to explore and exploit.

I wanted to write about some of these events, but with a twist. And so the Legion of The Damned was born; a Roman unit who would not be constrained by the usual rules of war. I wanted characters who would not necessarily act in the way disciplined Roman legionaries would have done: an expendable force of men who would be prepared to do whatever it took to complete their mission, as if their lives depended on it. Which, of course, they did. The Damned have nothing to lose and everything to gain.

It is perhaps pertinent to point out that, to the best of my knowledge, no such legion existed. Quite the opposite, in fact, because initially only property-owning Roman citizens aged between seventeen and forty-five were allowed to join the legions. As the Empire's borders expanded and their enemies increased, however, these rules were relaxed.

While the majority of the characters in this book are fictitious, some of those mentioned were real, including General Corbulo, who was sent by Emperor Nero to deal with the Armenian question. Control over Armenia was hotly disputed during this period of history. Both Rome and its eternal enemy, the Parthian Empire, the only other known power at that time which could confront Rome on an equal basis, sought to control Armenia either directly or through a puppet ruler. It is against this backdrop of simmering tensions that *Fortress of Steel* is set.

If you have enjoyed reading this book and have a few moments to spare, I would be truly grateful if you could write a review on **Amazon** and **Goodreads**. Reviews are the lifeblood of authors nowadays and are crucial for our success. I am also always keen to connect with my readers, and you can contact me via **Facebook**, **Twitter** or **my website**.

Jeff Jones

www.jeffjonesauthor.co.uk

SAPERE
BOOKS

www.ingramcontent.com/pod-product-compliance
Lightning Source LLC
LaVergne TN
LVHW091125080826
845145LV00008B/2050

* 9 7 8 0 8 5 4 9 5 6 8 7 6 *